Clever Canine Solutions

When 'Sit, 'Down', and 'Stay' are just not enough

Julie Hamilton Hindle

Clever Canine Solutions

Index of Exercises

Although many of these exercises are used to solve problems, there are many that are just for the fun of it. Enjoy!

Table of Contents

In this Chapter

Why I wrote this book

I wrote this book to encourage you the dog owner to think outside the box and for you to teach something a little different to your dog.

The book is written also for those of you who teach dog training classes on a regular basis. I know only too well the stress of having to teach classes week after week and the need to keep them fresh and come up with new exercises that will excite both dog and owner.

Perhaps you will find some extra activities that you have not thought of teaching before and add something new to your training, providing owner and dog with extra tools to help in developing their bond together.

I have not covered the basic training exercises in this book, i.e. Sit, Down, Stand etc., this book is designed to offer something beyond the basic building blocks. If any of the 'basic exercises' are needed to complete an exercise in this book, it will be highlighted at the beginning of each exercise in the box **Ace Top Trick**. It will say, if previous training is required. (More details on this at the end of this chapter).

The title **Clever Canine Solutions** came about because I wanted to offer something more than just 'tricks'. This book offers not just exciting exercises, but **solutions** to some common canine problems, through teaching your dog to use its brain to solve problems. Throughout the book you will find exercises that will provide extra mental stimulus for your dog to fulfil its potential as a truly 'clever canine'.

It all starts with a good foundation

All good structures must have a solid foundation. Foundation training is a very good place to start, before attempting more advanced exercises.

Foundation training provides the solid building blocks upon which all other training is built. However, if your dog already has the basics then this is the ideal point to pick up something new and exciting to add to their repertoire.

If on the other hand, you are struggling with your dog's behaviour and struggling keeping her focused on you, pick an exercise from this book that has the indicator **Ace Top Trick** at the top. Where it indicates **No Previous Training Required** and have a go at it. This might just be the kick-start that you and your dog need to develop a stronger bond and create the desire for your dog to focus and work with you regardless of the breed or how hard, people have told you, it will be to train them.

The idea is to teach simple, but fun exercises to encourage your dog to want to work with you and to stimulate your dog's mind. Your dog does not care what you teach them, and as long as, they are capable of learning what you choose, they will just love having your attention and bonding with you. They love nothing more than being guided and directed by a good leader, it is these very qualities that makes the dog, the wonderful companion they are.

The Trick to Problem Solving

The training methods used throughout this book are designed to encourage the dog to use their mind, to think and work things through. They are encouraged with positive reinforcement and their behaviour is shaped to suit the life-style needed for you, your family and for your dog, encouraging a more contented and fulfilled companion.

Using exercises that many would regard as mere tricks, we will teach exciting fun exercises that excite both owner and dog to want to learn them. For example, teaching the dog who barks too much, to bark on cue, so that she understands what she is doing and then the process can be reversed to teach her to be quiet. Or, the dog who jumps up when you come home, to teach her to walk backwards so that she gives you space rather than invading yours and jumping up when you are carrying shopping.

When I am training my dogs or teaching my classes, my aim is to keep exercises fresh and new for the dogs and the owners. Enabling learning and mental stimulation to occur.

It is my hope that this book will encourage you to think of other ways to keep your dog contented, stimulated and interested in being with you. It is written to encourage you to teach not just *Sit*, *Down*, *Stay* and *Come* — although these are important exercises — but there is much more your dog can learn, even from a very young age. I also want to encourage you, irrespective of your dog's age, for you both to learn new things together. It really is never too late for you or your dog!

Sometimes, the more an exercise stretches the dog mentally the more interested and motivated they are to learn and the more rewarding it is for you. To experience the joy of your dog's learning and development, to watch your dog get excited when she knows it's time to work with you is an absolute honour and a gift your dog will freely give to you.

At the beginning of each chapter, you will find an outline under the chapter heading titled, *In this Chapter*. This is for easy reference of what to expect in each chapter.

Teaching Dog Training Classes

At some point in many of the exercises you will find a box as at the end of this section, headed **Dog Trainer's Notes,** this is for you the Dog Trainer to offer a few pointers, they are merely meant as a guideline, for things to bear in mind, when teaching the exercises in your class, if you haven't taught it before.

I hope you find these helpful. For ease and quick reference, a black strip with **Dog Trainer's Notes** is written down the edge of the page to help you spot them quickly when thumbing through the pages.

As a dog trainer of 30 years practice, I became very aware of the importance of keeping my classes fresh and exciting both for dogs and their owners. I learnt that people practice much more at home when they are given a variety of exercises to practice. I also learnt that people practice far more when you give them exciting things to practice, rather than just the basic, normal exercises that we associate with dog training, such as sits and stays etc. As important as these exercises are, both owner and dog will become bored and tire, if this is all they practice for a whole week. My rule was to give the class a basic exercise and something a bit more exciting to take home and practice each week.

Understanding People

Training as an Adult Education teacher, opened my eyes enormously to how people learn and how disruptive some people can be in a class situation when they aren't understanding the trainer, or they have a dog who is proving challenging and they can't get to grips with it.

Dog training is in my opinion one of the hardest subject matters for people to learn. It is fact, that many people join dog training classes, not because they want to, but because they feel the need to. It is one of the few, perhaps even the only subject that a student will learn and teach simultaneously. People feel awkward, uncomfortable and vulnerable, having to try and emulate what the trainer is teaching them and in front of people they don't know. Keeping this in mind is advantageous to the success of your class. Being sensitive to each individual and their struggles within your class, is crucial. It does not matter if you are the best 'Dog Trainer' in the world, in a class situation your job is not to teach the dog, but to teach the owner to become their dog's trainer. People communication and enabling each owner to succeed with their dog is essential.

Making training fun for the owner to teach, is equally as important as it is, to make the training exercises exciting for the dog. If the owner doesn't enjoy what you are teaching you can bet their dog will miss out, as they won't be bothered to teach it.

The Importance of Homework

I am well-known in my dog training class for giving the class, too much homework to practice, rather than too little. My success rate was I believe, much higher because of this. For those that couldn't remember or couldn't fit it all in, in a week, (although many owners, got really good at note taking to ensure they didn't forget anything as they became more enthusiastic and enjoyed watching their dogs learn). And for those who were struggling with a particular exercise, it didn't matter that they achieved 'everything' each week, it all evened out in the end, but at least they practiced something and on the whole the achieved at least one of the exercises. This allowed them to experience the thrill as each week, they couldn't wait to show me what their dog had learnt. This was always the highlight of the week for me. I found it very exciting watching their faces as they demonstrated their achievements.

My classes were so varied and many of the exercises, people never dreamt their dogs would or could do, but they did. We seldom failed to achieve with a dog and owner on an exercise we set out to teach. My proud boast (if I'm allowed to say that), was that many of my clients taught such complex behaviours to their dogs, that some of those dog owners, would have been very good dog trainers if they had wanted to pursue it, many of these owners trained with me for many years.

Ace K9

I was very fortunate to fulfil a life-long dream of mine and in 2005 I opened a shop front 'Training, Behaviour and Grooming Centre' in Leigh-on-Sea, Essex. One of the first of its kind. By all accounts it was a very successful establishment, successful not because of the thousands of dogs that came through the doors, but successful because of the success/achievement rate.

You see, I was in a minority among dog training schools. I had a small training room at the front of my shop, where passers-by could happily observe the classes in action, and many did, other dog trainers would have been horrified at the space I trained in, but it worked exactly as I had planned.

Only four owners and their dogs per class, it was rather like private training and seldom did anyone leave my school without a trained dog. The exception being when they didn't prioritise attending the classes of course. On paper as a business plan, I was never going to be rich from this, but it was all about each dog achieving for me.

As a Dog Trainer, when your classes are small, everyone must achieve, there is no room for a dropout rate. You don't get to choose which owner listens best or who is the easiest to train, or which breed of dog you know you'll get the best result from. Every dog and every person matter, as a Dog Trainer and a Behaviourist, when somebody struggles or has a particularly difficult dog, for whatever that reason might be, my aim is to treat that person and dog as an individual and train them within that class until I find what works for them both. Whatever the exercise, there is always a way of making it happen, no matter what the breed of dog, unless you are asking for something they are physically not capable of, of course.

Dogs, regardless of the breed attending my training school, were all welcome. Those dogs that made it all the way to the advanced class, were so varied and seldom the typical collie that you expect to see at advanced level. I had everything from Boxers to Yorkshire Terriers and numerous Staffordshire Bull Terriers, when many trainers wouldn't even let them through their doors, let alone train them, yes, many training schools have a 'No Staffie ruling', without exception. The breed's reputation and the high volume of the breed, without a doubt dominated the area I lived in, in Essex at the time.

There was no 'typical' in my training school, when an owner entered through my doors, I saw dog rather than breed and believed all had the potential to become wonderful dogs and wonderful handlers given the right coaching.

All were welcome and the thrill of seeing any dog, reach a high level of training, was something else. I have worked with many, many aggressive dogs and many trained to amazing levels and for many their aggressiveness became a distant memory as they learnt to focus on the person in their lives. They had a purpose and felt secure and their brains where occupied. Most importantly, their owners understood them.

If you are a dog trainer reading this, then I know that you too care about the quality and variety of what you offer to the dogs and owners who come through the doors of your training school.

This book is not designed as comprehensive training manual but is written to provide you with some exercises that are not only useful in dealing with some unwanted behaviours that you may come across, but they are also fun to teach.

Ace Top Trick

Throughout the book, you will encounter two headings **Ace — Top Trick** and **Mr Tibs — Training Tips.**

Ace and Mr Tibs were just two of the very special dogs who taught me so much about being a dog trainer.

Ace was a German Shepherd + Northern Inuit, who came into my life in the same month that I was preparing to open the doors on a new dedicated Training, Behaviour and Grooming Centre — **Ace K9** — in 2005, which is where Ace took his name from.

Ace wasn't just my Best Friend, Mr faithful and Mr Reliable, he was also my working partner, teaching me and many other dogs just how good a friend a dog can be when raised correctly. He achieved more for helping to rehabilitate aggressive and nervous dogs in my behavioural sessions, than I could ever have achieved on my own.

I learnt from Ace to recognise better, a dog who was more likely to bite or who was more likely to attack another dog. He was 100% intuitive and accurate in his assessments.

One of my dogs, Beanie, came to me with her owner for a training session with some major aggressive tendencies, which triggered when she didn't get what she wanted. I was her  last chance as she was biting and attacking aggressively the people she lived with and visitors.

She doesn't know it, but Beanie owes her life and the fact that she is still here, to my golden boy Ace; because of his reactions to her, he showed me who she was; he is the reason she is still alive today and is very much loved and part of our family, even though she is still complex and, at times, hard-work!

Ace just did not feel she was a threat. He was comfortable around her, even when she was going for him, and launching herself at him. When he got too close to her space, he showed me everything she offered was through fear and insecurity and she really did not want to bite him, even when she was toppling her crate over and bouncing it across the floor warning him off, he still did not believe she was aggressive, and he was right.

He was a true gentle-giant and a friend to everyone he met, canine or human. The intensive training Ace had, created a true mediator he learned never to answer another dog back and avoid conflict. Except once when a Staffordshire Bull Terrier attached itself to the side of his face, he was perfectly justified in taking action to dislodge the attacker.

After eight short years with Ace by my side, I had to say good-bye to him. In February 2014 he lost his life to a cruel disease called Degenerative Myelopathy (DM), losing him left a huge gap in all our lives, I miss him every day and I still can't believe I no longer have him by my side, but my life is so much better for having had him in it.

Thank you for everything you gave me Ace, if I had the chance to do it again, I would do every single moment of the journey we had, minus the disease.

Mr Tibs Training Tips

I have been asked many times, why I chose the Tibetan Terrier, of all the breeds in the world that I could have chosen as a Dog Trainer? Hmmm?

The answer then and the answer now is the same, in my opinion all dogs have potential, and this was the breed who's potential I wanted to recognise.

Mr Tibs was my first Tibetan Terrier. I laugh every time I think about how much I thought I knew about dogs, until he came along, then I learnt very quickly that a Tibetan Terrier cannot be raised to be like a Labrador or a German Shepherd, well perhaps I should rephrase that, they can be raised the same, but the outcome may be different. There is a difference in how different breeds and different dogs react to different stimulus.

Things I learnt from Mr Tibs

✓ Mr Tibs taught me, I had to work extra hard if I was going to expect him to do the same.

✓ Tibs taught me to 'pay up' and 'pay well' if I expected him to work with me and for me.

- ✓ He taught me to lighten up and laugh when it all goes wrong, and it does not always matter when it isn't just perfect.

- ✓ Oh, and it is okay to change the order of the routine, even in front of a live audience. Ha! And he did just that.

- ✓ He taught me to enjoy dogs for exactly who and what they are and to appreciate their differences and that every day we have with them is a precious gift and a privilege.

- ✓ He taught me that no two dogs are the same, they think differently and what matters to each of them can vary enormously.

For all these reasons and more, I love the Tibetan Terrier and I learnt to appreciate and embrace any breed that came through my doors, and never to discriminate or make judgement calls on what they are capable of. Give every dog a fair chance, regardless of the breed and accept all for the wonderful animal that they are.

For these reasons, I have dedicated my life to living with this breed, amongst others.

I felt it only fitting that both Ace and Mr Tibs should play a part in sharing in the writing of my books, it is because of dogs like them, that I am able to share with you, all that they taught me.

Dog Trainer's Notes

In many of the exercises you will see a box, as on the following page, headed **Dog Trainer's Notes**, which is mainly for the Dog Trainer teaching in a class situation. They are offered as a quick guide for you of things to bear in mind when teaching the exercises to your class. I hope you find these helpful.

Encourage each member of your class to put together their own training bag that they will bring to class each week with their dogs. This way they won't forget any of their training props. The contents of the training bag could include:

1. Treat pouch
2. A Dog Toy (not a ball or squeaky toy)
3. Dumbbell or Retrieve object that is different from the toy.
4. A mat, *a cheap wipe-your-feet, door mat with rubber backing is ideal, not a full hearth rug. I once had a client bring a carpet that they had to carry over their shoulder! This is not necessary or convenient.*
5. The training bag will grow over time, to include a touch-stick, a cone. and possibly even a hula hoop, and a box.

How much you as a trainer or training school want to supply for your class, is your choice, some items are better to belong to individual dogs as they often won't use something with another dog's smell on it. For example, a mat and a dumbbell.

It is also a good idea to have enough of each of the props to go around the whole class. This means you can work all the class at the same time, rather than each having to wait in order to take a turn. There is also less standing around and more working for each person and dog, preventing boredom or frustration from setting in.

In this Chapter

o What if your dog was free to roam the streets?

o My wish-list for you and your dog

o Practice what you read

One of the privileges of being a Behaviourist is the invitation into people's homes, to work with families and their dogs. However, one of the most difficult parts for me is meeting a dog locked in a world where no one has taken the time to understand her, work with her and help her to reach her potential. I find this so sad and something that the dog has no control over, the dog is then given the label of being a 'delinquent dog', when all she is, is misunderstood.

Left to their own devices, they have no option but to get on with finding ways to relieve the boredom of each day. They use their brain in the only way they know how, by making up their own games of stealing, to get the owners attention, charging at high speed through the house and garden, negotiating objects on the way. Chewing on the walls, stairs and door-frames, re-landscaping the garden, escaping at every given opportunity, snapping and snarling at dogs while on the lead and my list could go on and on.

The worst part for me is, when the owner tells me, 'she is stupid or does not seem to understand when I have told her, No!'. The saddest part is that many of these dogs are often the cleverest of all dogs, they are struggling to fit in, and in a world, that is not theirs. A dog is a dog, and is not the same as us, dogs are not human — keep this always at the forefront of your mind, no matter how much you think they understand you. Our world is not the same as theirs and quite often not a lot happens for them on a day to day basis, when they live with us. Just because your dog lies sleeping for most of the day, whether you are at home or at work, doesn't mean they should. This can leave them struggling with the frustrations of the constraints they are bound to with no outlet for their mental or physical energy and their needs are simply not being met.

What if your dog was free to roam the streets?

What if your dog was not part of your family and was a member of a dog family living free, or lived a solitary life but free? Not all dogs live in packs in the wild. I am sure you would agree that their world would be very different. What would their world look like? Their appearance may not be too dissimilar to the dog in your home, as in the case with my main breed the Tibetan Terrier, as is seen from these photos of two dogs on the streets of Tibet.

At a guess, we would say, it would be sad if they were on the streets, because they would be dirty with no one to love them, never certain

where their next meal was coming from, and no comfortable bed to curl up on.

However, for them they would be free, making their own choices and the one thing that is almost certain, they would be busy. Busy, staying alive. Busy, making their own choices about when it's time to rest, when it's time to travel and when it's time to reproduce. They would be busy protecting their boundary, guarding their territory from intruders and busy searching for food. Most likely, scavenging amongst the bins and rubbish, rather than hunting for live prey, although for some that might also be an option, depending on the environment they lived in.

The one thing that is probably a guarantee, they would have no phobias, anxieties or behavioural issues. We, humans, on the whole, cause these things. Your dog would simply get on with living and doing what they need to do to survive.

So, which image creates the best picture for you? Living with us in our comfortable home, or living free doing what they want, even if it means struggling for food?

Hmm? as humans we can be very arrogant, we assume we know best, we assume that living with us simply must be the best thing, for whatever pet we choose to bring into our homes.

If being with us is the best thing for our dogs, then why is it so many cannot wait to escape the minute that front door is open? Why, when out on a walk do many dogs duck and dive when it is time to have their leads on? Why does your dog snap when you get too close to what is hers? If living in a house is so great, why do so many suffer with separation issues when we leave them? The answer to me is simple, their needs are not being met, or perhaps a trauma has happened, and they have been prevented from moving forward.

The dog may be domesticated, but they have needs, they have a brain, they have feelings, and they can and do become mentally frustrated and depressed when their needs are not being met.

Here is a thought for you to ponder. Just because your dog sleeps all day lying on the couch or in their bed without complaining, *does this mean they are happy?* It is very possible that your dog has no other option but to lie and sleep waiting for you to do something with them. This does not mean it is what they would like to do. It's easy to tell ourselves, 'She's alright, she's lying there contented and relaxed' Really? Think again. It is very possible that if your dog could speak, she may disagree.

My wish-list for you and your dog

1. It is my wish in this book, to take you on a journey with me, a journey that will hopefully inspire you to give your dog or the dogs you work with, something more to look forward to.

2. It is my wish for you that in learning to understand her better, you will help her to want to look to you, because you provide for her the extra stimulus and a companion she can trust and who gives her what she needs. Helping her to become a contented companion and helping her to avoid frustration and reach her full potential.

3. It is my wish for you that you will experience the pleasure I get, when my dog learns something knew and they start to do it before I have even asked them for it, because they think it is what I might want, and they are happy to please and engage with me.

4. If you have more than one dog at home, then my wish is that in teaching each of your dogs to share you and wait their turn, you will experience a rare reward of working with your dogs as a team.

Practice what you read

Having fun with your dog and working at engaging their minds that they may be receptive to learning, is an amazing experience and creates happy contented dogs that are a pleasure to live with.

Enjoy getting to know your dog's capabilities, unlock her world and help her to understand yours. Switching your dog on to you and her surroundings is what learning with my training is all about. It is my hope to help you, to discover your Clever Canine at their best, of course this can never happen without an owner who is prepared to put the work in.

It is no good reading a book and doing nothing with the information you receive. If you are not going to apply what you read in this book, then perhaps you might just as well stop reading now.

However, if you do pick up the baton and run with it for your dog, I would firstly like to congratulate you! Secondly, I would like to invite you, after you have read this book and worked it through or at least worked through some of it with your dog, to email me personally and share with me your experience of how you get on. Tell me what worked for you and what did not work for you, your opinions matter to me and I promise to read every message that comes to me.

Email: julie@acek9.net

Please note: Unfortunately, I cannot answer individual problems, but I can listen and learn from what works and what does not.

In this Chapter

o Just how clever is your canine?

o Which breed is the easiest to train?

Just how clever is your canine?

Just how clever are our canines? We each have our own answer to this I am sure, and I am certain the scientists will have their answers, some of which we might not like or want to hear. I believe that our dogs largely are a product of our making. What we do or do not do with them determines the outcome of the dog we will live with. So, when clients have said to me 'the dog is thick or stupid' (and yes, they do say it), I am often reminded of the phrase that Barbara Woodhouse coined 'There are no bad dogs, only bad owners'. Which I would paraphrase as, 'There are no stupid dogs!'

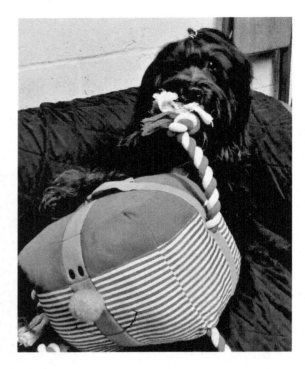

The training in this book is applicable to all breeds. I share my home with 6 dogs, 5 of whom are Tibetan Terriers, therefore I will make some reference to the Tibetan Terrier, or as they are affectionately referred to, as TT's for short. They are the breed who for the most part I share my home with.

No dog training is 'breed' specific in my opinion, but the TT is one of the breeds I have come to know and love alongside all the other dogs throughout my life. The TT can have a reputation for being stubborn, independent, aloof, cloth-eared, dominant, needy, pushy, determined, and bossy and sometimes even with an attitude. Flip the switch and they are funny, loving, clever, happy, friendly, busy, and an amazing all-round companion dog. This makes them a good reference point for me to refer to in this book, as they often prove a challenge for many unsuspecting owners.

The TT is no more difficult than any other dog, in my opinion, although some behaviourists may dispute this. Many times, they have and do prove to be a challenge for the new unsuspecting owner, who has purchased the Tibetan Terrier because they are cute and fluffy; I have even known other behaviourists to say they are difficult, and often impossible to get through to.

I have shared my home with the Tibetan Terrier breed for twenty-five-plus years, and currently live with five of them and a working sheepdog. My Welsh Working Sheep Dog I might add, is far more complex to live with (again in my opinion) than any of my TT's.

Which breed is the easiest to train?

I have been asked many times by many breeders and dog trainers, why I chose the Tibetan Terrier, when I could have chosen any other breed to live with as a dog trainer. I answered this in part, in the opening chapter, but the truth is, for me the Tibetan Terrier is a dog that I was attracted to when two of them walked into my training school one day, I was fascinated by them, every dog comes with its own breed tag, things that are unique to them, things that can make them a challenge, there is no 'easy' dog. When I first encountered the Tibetan Terrier, I never gave it a thought as to how well it would train, or what difficulties there might be with it. As a dog trainer, whatever dog I was presented with I would find a way of helping that dog to learn and I guess I felt the same about the Tibetan Terrier.

That also reminds me of a phrase I read in a Barbara Woodhouse book, way back when, I remember when someone asked her the question, "Which dog is the best breed to train?" She said, "The breed you want to own, choose the breed you want, because that's the dog you are most likely to train". Such an important decision, I have applied this throughout my life and have never owned a dog I could not or did not train.

Each of my Tibetan Terriers are as different as the next one, their personalities are different, their likes and dislikes are different, but one thing is consistent, they all love to learn, because they know how to learn. They all love to spend time with me and are chomping at the bit to see who it's going to be when I am getting ready to train. Their brains have been unlocked and they find their most contentment in being with me and working with me.

Whatever breed you have chosen as your companion, I would ask you 'not' to define them by their breed first. Define them as a dog first and their breed second, whether you have a Chihuahua, Great Dane, Beagle, Collie, German Shepherd, Boxer, Tibetan Terrier, or a mixture of whatever breeds you have chosen, if you define them by what the book says they can or can't do, you will block your dog from reaching his or her full potential.

Whatever their breed, train them. Teach them simple exercises and watch them grow and become a clever canine. All dogs have a brain, all dogs need to use their brains. They need to be stimulated, to have a job and a purpose, not to live locked behind four walls. Give your dog something to look forward to and watch her come alive, she will commit to you, when you commit to her. There is no greater feeling than when your dog would rather be with you than anyone else, because all good things come from you.

In this Chapter

o Corrective vs Positive Reinforcement Training
o Fair Pay
o What Makes Your Dog tick?

Whether you have a puppy or an adult dog that you want to train, introducing **Clever Canine Solutions** is a wonderful gift that you can give to him or her and the only cost to you, is what you paid for this book and the time it will take 'you' to learn the recipe and deliver the method.

Teaching your dog how to think and to use her mind, keeping her mentally stimulated which in turn produces a smarter, more contented and a willing to be with you dog. She will learn to think things through and work to receive each reward.

You could of course argue, 'should she have to work to receive her reward'? The honest answer is, she will be a much happier dog if she learns to work with you and receives stimulation in return. We are not making her work for her reward, because we are the boss, the more dominant one, or the dictator. We are encouraging her to work for her reward because by nature a dog would have to work to eat, they would have to hunt and find their food, before they would get to eat. Working for their reward, is the equivalent to your dog having a job, they will benefit from the stimulus and success in receiving the reward.

This is all part of understanding your dog. It is equally important that you take the time to understand what it is you are going to teach your dog with each exercise. The time that you spend, learning and understanding what it is you are going to teach, will speed the learning process up for your dog. Understanding will produce the results, not taking the time to understand, will lead to confusion for your dog and frustration for you both.

Corrective vs Reinforcement Training

All training sessions should be positive fun and happy. Reprimands and corrections have no place in dog training if you are to have a happy, willing companion.

Besides, always keep in your mind, 'You cannot correct a dog for doing something that she has not been taught, how can she possibly do it wrong if she has never been taught it.' If she is getting things wrong, look at yourself first and ask the question, 'Have I taught her what it is I want her to do? And what it is I do not want her to do'?

Each basic exercise you teach using these methods, will make it easier for her to learn the next one. As your dog learns how to think, they start to try to work things out for themselves because you have taught them how to use their minds and they now know how to learn.

It is so exciting the first time you pick up treats and your dog starts offering exciting behaviours in the hope that one of them might be what you want from her. I like to call this free-thinking. Once the dog has learnt how to learn, endless opportunities for you and your dog present themselves. Your journey is just beginning!

Fair Pay

Throughout the book I will refer to your dog's treats or rewards as payment, she does a job for you and you pay up for it. You would do well to keep in mind, many dogs place different values on what is worth working for. For example, some dogs like the Labrador, may work for dog kibble/meal, for many dogs like the Tibetan Terrier, the payment value may need to be much greater, meat, ham, sausage, perhaps even liver etc. but every dog is different, so you will need to test out what matters to your dog.

Every dog has something that matters to them, something that they value and will see as worth working for. Your job is to find out what that is, I hear from many people who tell me, 'My dog is not food orientated', look at what you are offering them, or the time you are offering it. Are they hungry? How well fed is your dog?

You may also find different environments will make a difference to what your dog will work for, for example. Within your home, your dog may work for any dog treat, but take her to the park and you may have to up the stakes. This may mean providing something with a stronger scent or taste, like sausage or even liver. This is because the distractions are far greater outdoors and more exciting to her, you will be competing with the sights, sounds and smells of the environment.

You need to make yourself as attractive to her as possible, you must help her want to choose you, over the distractions of the environment. Sights, sounds and smells all become your competition; your job is to win this competition so that your dog wants to be with you more than anyone or anything else. It is your job to help create this mind-set.

What Makes Your Dog Tick?

Every dog is different, what matters to one may not matter to the next. For example, take my breed the Tibetan Terrier, out of my five Tibetan Terriers, only two of them would remotely consider working for a toy, but that is not to say that 'yours' may not prefer the toy. You need to know what it is your dog considers worth working for. She must want the treat you have on offer if she is to consider working with you. They need to see it as worthwhile and will make it very clear if you have not got it right, particularly when they are younger, and you are working at developing the bond with them. Your dog, whatever their breed, may fall into this category too, so it will be trial and error to see what works best.

Different breeds of dogs have evolved over many years, for different reasons and purposes. For example, gundogs & hounds use their noses, the desire to hunt by scent is often much more important than paying attention to their owner. However, if you train your dog well, you can put their desire to sniff to your advantage by having strong smelling treats on offer, this can often be enough to create their desire to work. On the other end of the scale, working breeds such as the German Shepherd Dog, Collie or the Boxer, would often sell their soul for the simplest of toys and interaction with their owners over food, food may be second on their list of preferences, of course in either category, there is always the exception to the rule.

My sheep dog Beanie, will work for either toy or food, but if you want speed and constant commitment from her on an exercise, then the toy is always her best stimulator, food slows her down (although by most dog's standards it is still fast) and her attention is not held for quite as long. However, her precision may be greater with food because her excitement level is more controlled. So, the payment I use at the time, will be determined by the exercise I want to teach her, or the exercise I want her to complete.

Mr Tibs—Training Tips

Very few TT's will want to work for dog food / kibble. Certainly not in the early days of training. Dog treats are not ideal either. You are going to feed a high volume of treats in the early stages. So, you will need to mix it up a bit to keep their interest and to prevent tummy upsets.

Learning what makes 'your dog' tick and what is important to your dog is essential. As I said, you can only learn this by trial and error. So, get experimenting. Even different foods will create different results.

Fed in volume, 'dog treats' are more likely to cause upset tummies and cause your dog to gain weight, for this reason, using dog treats for training is best kept to the occasional exercises taught at home, never use them in a training class situation.

High value treats for most dogs might include: ham, cheese, sausage, chicken, beef, liver cooked or freeze-dried are all good and I would regard any of these as high value payment treats, but it's not my opinion on them that counts, it is your dog's that matters.

If you want the best from your dog, be prepared to pay well. The value of what you pay will often determine your dog's efforts for you. Certainly, if it's a breed like the Tibetan Terrier, you may have to put some effort into what you offer them.

You would not work for free, and neither should your dog have to, 'Pay up and Pay well', give your dog what your she deserves, that is if you expect her to want to work with you.

In this Chapter

- o Becoming bilingual
- o Our flexible friend
- o Things you should know and remember about a dog
- o Give your dog what she needs, not what you think she needs

Becoming bilingual

You and your dog have your own language and you would do well to consider yourself foreign to him or her. To live together successfully, it is important that you learn to understand each other's lingo.

There is no doubt in my mind that our dogs learn to read our body language, better and faster than we read them, which is quite ironic, given that we are supposed to be the more superior species. The dog's language, physical and verbal, consists of signs, signals and sounds. If you haven't done so already, it would be extremely helpful to 'your dog', if you became familiar with what she is saying to you, both verbally and with signals 'now', particularly if you would like this relationship to develop well. It is much easier for you to learn to speak 'dog', than it is for her to learn the 'human' language. Although I have met, many dogs that learn faster than their owners do.

You, can read it all for yourself, far greater people than I have studied the dog and documented their behaviour, for many, many years and made it available for you and me, to read and understand. You are not reliant upon your dog or someone else to teach you. Your dog on the other hand is 100% reliant upon you learning and becoming a good teacher, this can take time, but your patience with her will be rewarded. Your dog has all the time in the world for you, it is always a good thing if we repay some of this patience.

Does your dog speak your language?

Learning to speak your language, your dog will try to interpret or apply what you do and how you behave in relation to her own world. For example, if she puts her teeth on you and you pull away from her or remove your hands from her every time, she may use this as her way to control contact from people that she does not want to touch her. In the dog world, the weakest submits, by either walking away or freezes when they feel under pressure.

She needs to learn to play with her humans in a different manner than she would with her dog friends, we are not able to play in the same way she would with her own kind. She knows you are not a dog, so do not try to be one. You would do well to remember she is not human, no matter how much you want her to be, it just is not going to happen. Keeping this in mind prevents problems from developing along your journey together and shows respect for her as the wonderful animal she is.

Our flexible friend

Fortunately, dogs are very capable of learning and fitting into another way of life and behaving overall, the way we want them to. They are by far our most flexible and versatile friend.

No matter what job they have evolved to do, they can learn to adapt to many others. Her adaptability is what makes the dog the wonderful companion and the ideal pet that we know. She is the only animal  that has been domesticated to such a degree and despite all the mistakes we make with her and all the horrible ways she is treated, she

is still able to remain trusting, accepting, loyal and flexible. Wow, do we have a lot to learn from her.

Things you should know and remember about a dog

1. She is never resentful, nor does she hold a grudge, (despite what you might think). Humans are the only ones who exhibit such behaviours.

2. She does not instinctively know what you mean. When she is not getting it right, it is usually because she does not understand what it is you want her to do, most likely you have not taught her properly, if at all.

3. She does not plan a head.

4. She is not out to get you, by doing things just to upset you, despite what it may look like to you. These thoughts too, are human thoughts and could not be further from how your dog thinks.

5. Learn to speak your dog's language, don't expect her to come into your home bi-lingual.

Invest Wisely

Put nothing in and you will get nothing back. You would do well to consider your dog as a good investment; you only get out what you put in. Dogs generally repeat what is worth it to them; they generally do not repeat what brings a negative experience.

Therefore, if when your dog steals your cushions of the couch you go running after her, chasing her around the garden, you can be sure she is going to repeat this behaviour, since it brought attention and fun the first time, she won't care what you are shouting at her, she will find your attention rewarding. Your reaction now sets the precedence for her to repeat the behaviour. Even though you might have thought you were telling her off, she will see it as positive attention and often for many, some attention is better than no attention, just as with children.

Give your dog what she needs, not what you think she needs

Dogs have needs, just like you and me. It is important that you recognise this when you decide to bring a dog into your life. When you take a dog into your home you enter a relationship, it is important that this relationship is not one-sided.

It is not enough that you get a dog to be there to greet you when you come home from work and offer her a walk round the block in the morning and the same on your return.

It is not enough that the children want a dog, so she sits at home all day to await their return, in the hope they can be bothered to play with her after school.

It is not enough that your dog should eat a vegetarian diet because that is what you eat, they need meat, well you can probably conjure up a vegetarian diet and she will survive, but it's not what she would choose, it's not what she would want. Do the test if it makes you feel better. Set a bowl of vegetables down and a bowl of meat down in front of her and watch which one she chooses.

It is not enough that you have a large garden, so she never needs to go out, or the back door remains open, so she can run in and out all day, so therefore she must be contented.

It is not enough that she lies and sleeps all day without causing a problem for you. This doesn't mean she is happy and it doesn't make it ok to do nothing with her.

It is not enough that you allow your dog free run of the house and to sleep on your bed, cook her steak, dress her in clothes or provide any other luxuries for her and expect her to understand that these things are important to her, because they are not.

None of the above points, provide for the physical and mental wellbeing of a dog. A dog needs the 'correct food', water, shelter, exercise both physical and mental, companionship, direction and affection, if they are to become a healthy, balanced and socially acceptable pet. It is your job to meet all these needs to consider yourself a good dog owner. Companionship is a two-way street, it's not enough that your dog is a companion to you, you need to be a companion to them too.

They are 'a dog', and no matter how hard you try to make it happen, she will never become your baby. You will do your dog an enormous favour if you keep this in mind. I am sorry if I am repeating myself on this point, but I make no apology if this seems harsh, as I am saying this on behalf of all the dogs whose homes I have visited who are displaying aggression, anxieties and/or phobias, because they are so misunderstood and treated in a way that doesn't fulfil their needs.

It is heart-breaking when after ½ hour of meeting a dog in their home, they come and sit by my feet and I know if I walked out the door with them on a lead, that they would never look back. If you cannot or do not want to meet these needs, then perhaps having a dog is not the pet for you.

If after reading this book one person makes the decision, that a dog is not for them, then I have done my job and prevented another rescue dog from occurring. If on the other hand, you still want a dog after reading this, congratulations! You have the makings of a fantastic dog owner.

NOTES

In this Chapter

o A word about manners
o Naming/shaping behaviours
o How does your dog see it?
o Manners in the home
o What is a Zoomie?
o What is in it for the dog?
o Puppy Zoomies

A word about manners

Good manners are essential if you are all to get along, but a dog has no concept of what are good, or bad manners — these are human terms. However, since it's what we humans understand, I will use it to refer to how we would like the dog in our homes and our society to behave. Consistency from you is essential if your dog is to understand what it is you want and where she fits in, within the family and society. From the moment, she enters your world the teaching process should begin. From day one, she will be looking to know what her role is and what you mean when you speak to her. It must be a very confusing and frustrating environment for a dog that has not been taught, what is expected of her and she is constantly told off for something she has no concept of the meaning.

Mr Tibs — Training Tips

- Set guidelines and boundaries
- Decide where your puppy is allowed and where she is not and stick to it.
- Upstairs – it is best kept off limits, in the early months to begin with.
- Anywhere where there is carpet should be off limits, until completely toilet-trained.

If you keep shouting, 'NO!' at your puppy, but do not follow through and show her what it is you want her to do, the chances are she will keep repeating the behaviour. She will start to show her frustration by barking and growling at you if you do not help her to get it right, by ending with a positive, rather than constant negatives.

For example, your puppy is chewing on the edge of your sofa and you shout 'NO!' You remove her from the sofa area and when you let her go, she goes straight back to it. This time you shout 'NO!' louder and remove her again, by the third time, your puppy is anticipating you coming, she runs off and then turns to bark or growl at you, so what has your puppy learnt?

She has learnt that chewing on the couch, makes you very loud and animated which creates excitement or anxiety for her. What you have not done is taught her what it is you want her to chew on. So always, when you are with your puppy, make sure you are armed with a suitable dog chew or toy, so that the next time she decides to chew what she shouldn't, make a noise or sound ehh, ehh, or growl. If she looks at you, either give her the 'Yes' word, or tell her she's a 'Good Girl' straight away, ('Yes' and 'Good Girl' are reinforcement for stopping chewing the couch at that moment), at the same time offer her the alternative to chew on, which is the dog chew or toy.

If she chooses to go back to the couch a second time, you must repeat the same process, sometimes a loud clap of your hands can be enough to stop them in their tracks, but you must immediately reward her when she stops with 'Good Girl' and work to get her attention on to the chew. What you have taught her through this process is, that chewing on the couch is not acceptable but there is an alternative and the happy tones of 'Yes' or 'Good Boy/Girl' and a chew or toy presented to her, are the positives in stopping what she was doing and therefore it is worth her while to stop.

Naming/shaping behaviours

One of the easiest ways to teach your dog what words mean is to say them as it happens. When she sits, say 'Sit', when she is going out, say 'Out' or 'Outside'. This method of shaping can be used, to help with solving some undesirable behaviours that a dog may be exhibiting. If you put the behaviour that you want to stop on a cue first, so that the dog understands it when you say it, you can then reverse what it is you want them to do, to stop the behaviour completely, or control and minimise the behaviour. Let me explain further.

If you have a dog who likes the sound of her own voice and barks a lot, then teach her a name for what it is she is doing. So, if you teach her that the word 'Speak' means she can bark, then reversing this behaviour becomes so much easier, because she understands what it is she is doing.

Another example, if you have a dog that bolts through that open door at every given opportunity, you can teach her that only when she hears the word, 'Go' or 'Out" can she exit from it. You can also block the desire to run through doors by teaching her to 'Back up', away from the door before you enter through it or before you open it.

Throughout the book, we will teach the dog that certain things she sees or wants, needs a particular result from her, before she will receive it. For example, when her dinner is being prepared, your dog goes to her bed or a mat, and remains calm, before it is presented to her.

How does your dog see it?

Overall dogs are not complicated, my experience of 30 years working in the behavioural field has taught me that dogs are for the most part predictable, treat them a certain way and you will get a certain result. Even the dog who bites someone, there is always a trigger, signs and signals to say the dog is feeling under threat, challenged, scared and uncomfortable. Just because you did not see the bite coming does not mean she did not give you a signal. Some signs are obvious, and others may be harder to spot.

Did you know that when a dog yawns it does not always mean she is tired? Sometimes a yawn can mean the dog is under stress. Recognising the difference between a stress yawn and a tired yawn would be a huge start. If you knew this sign, you could remove the pressure from your dog before she feels the need to take it to the next level.

Manners in the garden

Your garden should not be given over to your dog to use as she likes, if you are to have any say over it in the long run. I am always amazed at how many people ask me, 'How do I stop my dog digging the garden up'? If your dog is left with free access to the garden and can wander around whenever she wants, she is therefore free to do what she wants with it, this includes digging and pulling up the plants, as far as she is concerned. You can't give her it and say to her, 'Now you are not allowed to dig, or pull the plants up, chew the decking or the kid's toys etc.' She just won't get it. If you allow her free access, without supervision, in her mind, you have given the space to her and she will make it home by doing what she wants with it. Therefore, you might as well get over that, if you want her to have free reign of it OR, you can draw new boundaries.

My dogs have always had a pen, immediately outside the rear of the house, this allows the dogs access to go out for fresh air and to toilet, but they cannot access the garden area. The garden is my area and the only time they are in it is when I open the gate for them and invite them in.

They have *zoomie* times most days in the garden and of course training sessions. They are not allowed to toilet on the grass at home and they are taught that they must go back to their toilet area (the pen) if they need to go. This works well, as I do not have to do poo patrol before using the garden, the grass is not going to be destroyed by urine burning, although the sun has taken care of that this year, but there is no destruction of the garden, (except for tread-marks from speed running around it, and the occasional flattened bush or flowers from running through them).

This means we are all able to enjoy it, it also means I do not have ill dogs, from not knowing what they have eaten when left unattended in the garden. However, if you are one of those people that believes your dog should have access to the garden whenever she wants, then don't be upset when she re-landscapes it for you, she is only making it her own because you gave it to her.

Manners in the home

Your home is 'your' home and your dog is, invited in to share it with you. It is never your dog's home for her to do what she wants with it, otherwise you open the door for problems to arise and soon a behaviourist is knocking on your door, you will need them to solve the unwanted behaviours. Therefore, restrictions are essential to teach your dog where she fits in to the grand scheme of things.

It is essential that you remember from the previous chapter, 'She is not a human, she is a dog', no matter how much you think of her as your baby, she is an animal fur baby, not a human baby, and you will confuse her and cause problems for her if you forget this important matter.

Restricting your dog's movements is essential in the early days if things are to go smoothly and problems avoided. Setting the boundary lines from the beginning, allows your relationship to develop and the boundary lines can move later, if that is what you want.

Omitting to create boundaries in the beginning is a big mistake, as your dog is quite likely to see the house as hers and you as her guests, rather than the other way around.

What are Zoomies?

Also referred to as the mad-half-hour. The zoomie is the term I use to describe, when the dog zooms around as fast as their little legs will go, negotiating objects on route, albeit jumping over your furniture, under or over the coffee table, off the walls, round the tree and through your favourite flower bed. This all takes concentration and  calculated risks so that an injury does not occur. You will often hear it described as the 'mad-half-hour'.

Many people will describe this behaviour as being at its worst approximately an hour and a half after dinner time, this usually happens because the dog has had an adrenaline surge caused by food going into the body, so they have more energy.

For some dogs these sessions can be quite extreme and often appear quite aggressive, for many of us and in particular people like myself with multiple dogs, we will seldom notice it, or I should say take much

50

notice of it, as the young dog will usually direct it's attention and needs, to play with another dog. However, I have gone into many homes where dogs display this seemingly aggressive behaviour and believe it or not it can manifest itself as quite aggressive from some puppies, particularly as they grow with age.

What is in it for the dog?

For many people, they see this as the dog just having fun, perhaps because it just looks like they are happy and having a good time. My opinion on this is, it is a natural letting-off steam mechanism, it releases tension and drains physical and mental energy, and it would be a good tool in aiding your dog to perfect, his or her chasing and perhaps catching a meal if she needed to, in the wild.

Whatever the reasons for your dog enjoying this behaviour, I believe that the most important and logical reason is, that it is the dog's natural mechanism for draining mental energy and letting off steam. Watch closely the next time your dog does it and be in awe of the skill and precision needed to perfect the manoeuvres of going over, under and around objects and even avoiding being caught by another dog or you when they are playing or avoiding banging into an object.

When is a Zoomie a problem?

Often when I have been called into a home, for a behavioural visit, the zoomie has become out of control, because the owner does not understand it and is trying to stop the dog from displaying this seemingly 'crazy' behaviour. The dog not only runs at full speed but is also grabbing at anything in her path as she goes, this may even include the owner. It can become quite unnerving for some people and it is almost impossible to catch a dog when they have mastered the zoomie and to be honest, I cannot imagine why you would want to.

Most dogs, at some point in the day, need to do this, particularly when young, although my 14-year-old a couple of times a week, launches into the zoomie. The zoomie can occur at any time, but quite often early evening is a favourite, usually an hour or so after eating. Although mine usually do it at least once out on their run with one another.

It is a good idea, to either train your dog at their zoomie time, or simply take her into the garden and let her exercise this need, to tire her mind. Do not let her make you part of her circuit, stand well out of the way and keep children out of the way and enjoy the spectacle while keeping an eye out for any objects that might be hazardous to her route.

Puppy Zoomies

Many puppies start doing zoomies from a very young age, there is nothing wrong with this, it is part of their development and learning, if it is contained in a safe environment, and control is  maintained. It is also important that your dog is not displaying the zoomie due to frustration from lack of exercise or stimulus.

Where possible do not allow your puppy to do this indoors through the house, or round the living room, this is a very bad practice to encourage in a puppy. Remember puppies grow up and when your full-size dog is bouncing of the furniture and grabbing everything in her path, it will no longer be cute, and you will regret it, particularly if you have children at home. It is better that you block this behaviour indoors now, but do not deny them it. Learn to recognise when it happens and provide the appropriate area for it.

Some young dogs can develop quite a nasty streak at this hyper-time and become quite intimidating to some members of the family, usually because the puppy becomes frustrated at trying to stimulate play and interaction from someone. For many the only response they get is laughing and screaming, (particularly if children are around), which adds to the already heightened excitement, adding justification for the puppy to continue exhibiting this behaviour. Then the puppy grows up and the laughing owner no longer finds it funny.

When a young dog is going through adolescence, it is not unusual for her to return from her hour-long walk only to go straight into doing zoomies when the lead is removed at home. This is because the walk you have taken her on provided physical stimulus, but very little mental stimulus. It is estimated that approximately 5% to 10% of the brain is used mentally when out on a walk, this percentage is used for reading the messages left by other dogs by sniffing, unless of course, you train your dog during walk time, then they will use considerably more of their brain and be far more contented.

As I said, 'The Zoomie' is your dog's way of mentally tiring herself, which will leave her sufficiently tired and content enough to allow her to settle and sleep. It is probably a good idea when you come home from a walk, to take your dog out in to the garden and allow her to exercise her zoomie, if this is something she normally does after walking, rather than risk her doing it inside, or better still spend 5 to 10 minutes training her. Then put her to bed and know that she will sleep contentedly. Do not put her to bed to prevent the zoomie, as she will be a very frustrated dog. Most dogs once they have completed the zoomie will lie down and go into a good sound-sleep, as they will be physically <u>and</u> mentally exhausted after it. Remember the next time your dog or puppy starts charging around at full throttle and looks like she's losing it, it's just a zoomie and perhaps she needs something more to content her, or maybe she simply needs to let off steam before she can have a good sleep.

I have been dealing with this natural behaviour, that virtually every puppy goes through, for many years. When it goes out of control, it is no longer fun for anyone, fortunately for most it doesn't reach this stage, although it is wise to be aware and remember if you don't want it as a full-grown dog, be careful of encouraging it in your puppy.

Free access to the garden is just not enough

Being locked in a world where, you are expected to amuse yourself, on a day to day basis and then get told off because you have chewed up the remote control or  dug a crater in the garden or pooped on the couch rather than outdoors when you were left alone to play, must be very frustrating for the dog and personally I think it is very unfair.

Just because you leave the back door open all day or provide a dog-flap and your dog can come and go freely to explore it, does not create contentment for her.

If there is nothing going on for your dog to concentrate on, they will make up their own entertainment, to relieve the boredom and frustration, by digging, chewing, and worst-case scenario self-mutilating and most likely displaying zoomies.

NOTES

In this Chapter

o It's <u>all</u> relevant

o Exercises that do not require props or equipment

  Catch, Give Paw, Flat and Over, Turn-around,

  Walk backwards, Head Down, and Head Up, Quiet Please

It's <u>all</u> Relevant

It does not matter what you teach your dog, whether it is sit, lie down or jumping through hoops, it is all relevant to your dog. They simply enjoy learning, whether you view the exercises as tricks or simply more complex exercises, does not matter. Do not get hung up on what you should or should not be teaching your dog, she will love working with you, no matter what you teach her. My experience is the more complicated the exercise the more excited they are to do it.

Dogs get bored, very quickly learning sits and downs, waits and stays, as I said earlier. In my training classes, my aim is having dogs and owners practice as much variety as they possibly can. I have had people achieve exercises they never dreamt would be possible with their dog. The more variety you have to learn the more you will practice and the less bored you and your dog will be.

The following exercises are great for communicating desired and undesired behaviours from your dog, as well as being fun to teach and great fun for your dog to learn as well as being useful.

These exercises do not need equipment

1. Catch

2. Paw

3. Flat and Over

4. Turn around

5. Walk backwards

6. Head Down, Head Up

7. Quiet Please

Catch

Believe it or not, not every dog can catch a treat or a ball, in fact some dogs find it difficult, but it doesn't mean you can't try to teach it. I have taught many dogs to catch

Ace—Top Trick Catch
A problem solver
A 'Sit' is a good position for your dog to know, before learning this exercise.

when their owners had thought it wasn't possible. Although there have been one or two that I have not achieved it with. The two dogs that I can think of, a Bichon and a Wire-haired Fox Terrier, were both frightened by the treat coming towards them. It was as though you were throwing rocks at them, quite amusing at the time, both dogs would close their eyes when you threw the treat to them, they just didn't want to know.

The Fox Terrier (Toby) would even run away when he saw your hand prepare to throw. It wasn't a big issue as it was the only thing he didn't like, so we didn't push the issue.

Teaching 'Catch' as a Problem Solver

From a training point of view, it is a great exercise to teach as it:

Ace—Top Trick 'Catch'

Sit and Down are good positions for your dog to know before learning this exercise.

You will need: your dog and plenty of treats.

o Saves time if you can throw the treat to the dog and not have to go back to the dog to reward it.

o If the dog can catch. then it means she doesn't have to move out of position to go searching for the treat on the floor.

Greedy dogs generally learn to catch faster than others, as they are so desperate to get that piece of food. Never met a Labrador who couldn't catch! Tibetan Terriers sometimes struggle with it, often the hair over their eyes, when they jump to catch the treat will move and cloud their judgement, basically, the hair moves and blinkers their eyes, so it is important to make sure their hair is well tied back. Having said that, my best catcher is my Tibetan Terrier Mosi, she seldom misses, and her daughter Amara is somewhat impressive at catching too.

How to teach Catch

(1) Have your dog sit in front of you so that you can aim for the mouth when you throw.

Your aim is very important, so

it will take a bit of practice on your part. Initially when you start throwing, the dog may not make any effort, she may simply sit and wait for the treat to fall to the floor. Just keep asking them to sit and keep trying, you will suddenly see or hear their mouth move and you will know at this stage, they are thinking about it and thinking about catching it before it hits the floor.

(2) When you see your dog's mouth move say "Yes" so that she starts to connect what you are looking for.

Make the treat big enough that the dog can see it clearly. Small cubes of cheese are good for this or sausage. Ham is no good as it is too light to throw and tends to stick to your fingers.

Each dog will vary on the effort they put into catching their prize treat. Some will barely move off the spot, and wait until the treat is within easy reach, others like Mosi, in the photo, will throw their heart and soul into catching their prize.

(3) When she catches her first piece, give a huge cheer and praise her to let her know that she's done what you want. Lots of practice and she'll soon be a pro at it. Practice makes perfect.

Paw—Left, and Right

All dogs learn to give their paw at some point, often by default.

Giving paw is the one exercise that most owners attempt to teach their dog, Why? Probably because it's seen as a friendly gesture.

It is also an exercise that the dog will opt to use to get your attention.

Most owners enjoy their dog doing this, which is probably why most dogs use it and learn it so quickly

How to Teach Paw

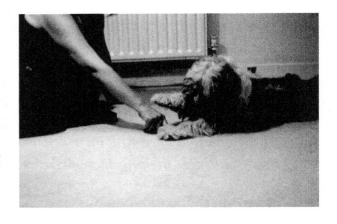

(1) Begin with your dog in a Down, if possible. (If your dog can't do a Down, don't worry, ask for a Sit instead).

(2) Kneel on the floor at your dog's level. If your dog is in a Down place your hand on the floor in front of her.

Your dog will sniff at your hand, trying to locate the treat.

When she can't retrieve the treat from sniffing and pushing your hand, she will try pawing at your hand.

(3) As soon as her paw contacts your hand, say 'Yes' to mark the behaviour as what you want and reward her straight away with the treat from your hand.

Keep repeating it until she becomes consistent at pawing your hand. Reward every time.

Now that your dog is touching your hand each time you present it on the floor it's time to move the goal posts, again.

Keeping your dog in a Down raise your hand off the floor and present it in front of your dog's face, still with treats in it.

Hopefully your dog will lift her paw and reach up to touch it.

At this point, huge excitement should erupt with a very happy 'Yes', letting your dog know that, that is exactly what you are looking for.

Repeat a few times until she is consistent in reaching up to touch your hand.

It's now time to introduce the cue, 'Paw'. As your dog touches your hand, say 'Paw'. You are now telling her what this is called. As with all the exercises, you only need to say the word as she is doing it, not before, at this stage in the training.

Time to move the goal posts, yet again!

(4) Ask your dog to Sit, and with a closed fist full of food, take your hand to the dog's nose and ask her for 'Paw', pause for a second and see what happens.

If training has gone well, your dog should offer her paw without hesitation.

I teach my dogs Left Paw and Right Paw. I do this by offering alternate hands to each paw. As a rule, I don't encourage the dog to cross it's paws over to the same hand as I think this is less tidy and more complicated when the dog is working beside you instead of in front of you.

(5) So, with the dog sitting in front of you offer your right hand for your dog's left paw and left hand for right paw. This keeps things tidy and consistent for the dog.

It's now time to move from having the treats in your hand.

Put a treat into one hand and keep it out of reach from your dog.

With the other hand offer the closed fist as before for the dog to contact.

As soon as your dog lifts her paw, open your hand allowing the paw to contact your palm.

Say 'Yes' to mark the behaviour and reward straight away.

Repeat until she becomes consistent at putting her paw in your hand and you no longer need to make a fist

Repeat for both left and right paw.

It is a good idea at this stage, to introduce the cue Left Paw, Right Paw. Say the words only as the dog is offering the behaviour.

Once the dog becomes consistent and lifts her paw when you offer a hand, you can start pre-empting it with the cue, 'Left Paw' or 'Right Paw'.

Flat and Over

Why Teach Flat and Over?

Along with the sit and down, flat and over is one of the first exercises I teach my puppies, in fact it is one of the first exercises I teach in every training class.

It teaches your pup to trust you and the environment you are both in.

They learn that nothing bad is going to happen because they lie in a submissive position in public, or around other dogs.

They are learning to trust and relax in the ultimate submissive position when you ask them to.

Benefits of Flat and Over as a problem-solver

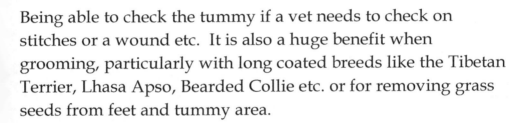

Ace—Top Trick

A Problem Solver

Your dog should be able to do a reliable Down before starting this exercise. As with every exercise, teaching should begin with small steps.

Being able to check the tummy if a vet needs to check on stitches or a wound etc. It is also a huge benefit when grooming, particularly with long coated breeds like the Tibetan Terrier, Lhasa Apso, Bearded Collie etc. or for removing grass seeds from feet and tummy area.

How to teach the Lie Flat

(As a trick, it is often called 'Play Dead' — not a phrase I like to use!)

The dog should never, be forced over onto its side, doing this would break your dog's trust in you instantly, and make her suspicious of your intentions.

The exercise should look like this. Down, Flat, back to a Down then over to the opposite side, (see photos in step by step).

Down

Step by Step

(1) With a handful of treats in your hand, have her lie down with her belly on the floor. (You should have already taught this before beginning the Flat and Over exercise).

The 'trick' to this exercise is teaching her to turn her head to the side, so that she will shift her weight onto one hip without you having to physically touch her.

Trying to force your dog onto their side will cause many dogs to resist and become anxious about what you are asking them to do, many dogs can see this as quite threatening, so take your time and earn their trust.

(2) Place the treat to the side of her nose just enough so that she will turn her head a little. Give her the treat as soon as she turns her head. Once you give her the first treat, see if you can follow with several more treats, before she moves her head back to a different location. This will require holding several treats in the treat hand at once to reward in quick succession. Do this 5-10 times.

(3) The next time hold the treat further to her side so that she turns her head more towards her back/shoulder.

With each step, lure with the treat so that she turns her head more. Soon she will turn her head enough so that she rolls over onto her hip and then she will lie on her side.

(4) Once on her side, give a string of treats. Hold the treat low enough so that she remains on her side. At first have the sequence of treats come frequently, and then increase the interval between treats so that she learns to stay in that position for longer amounts of time for the same number of treats. You can even have her lie on her side for extended periods,

(5) When you get to the point that it is easy to present a treat and have her immediately lie on her side, introduce whatever word you want her to associate as the cue word for it. My cue word is 'Flat'; remember to pay well once she is lying on her side. Multiple rewards as payment in quick succession will encourage her to stay in the position longer. Introduce a hand signal and make it clear and consistent.

(6) Once I have taught the dog to lie on one side, I teach the dog to go onto their opposite side using the exact same steps. I like to give a separate name to this side, so that the dog can differentiate which side you want her to lie on, I cue this as 'Over'.

Gradually increase the length of time you ask her to stay on her side, before paying up. Remember not to lose her 'Down' in the process and excitement of the new 'exercise'.

> **Important**: Do not roll the dog over, to get her to go on the other side, they must come back to a Down and then switch sides. 'Roll Over' is a whole different exercise we will learn this later. It is important to learn 'Flat' and 'Over' first, before 'Roll Over' or 'Flat' and 'Over' will be much harder to teach.

Turn Around

Why Teach Turn Around?

A simple exercise to teach and you will be amazed at how useful it is. Great for when you are bathing, grooming and for examination on the vet's table.

I also had a dog that went blind and I was so glad that I had taught him this exercise in his early days, it got him out of many sticky spots.

Ace—Top Trick
No previous training required

A Problem Solver
Useful for grooming or in the bath or at the vets, or for teaching the trick reversing through legs.

How to Teach the Turn

(1) With your dog in front of you, take a treat to her mouth and have her follow it in a half circle in either direction, until she is facing the opposite direction to where she was standing. Pay her with a few treats in quick succession.

If she is reluctant to follow the treat, pay her first just for moving her head in the direction you want her to move.

This exercise must be broken down, as much as is necessary to encourage the dog to move to get the reward. It is important to pay them for effort.

Repeat 5 to 10 times until she is moving more freely.

(2) Once she starts to follow the treat with no effort, introduce your word 'Turn', as she is moving.

The aim is for her to turn as soon as you say the word and point to a direction.

(3) Get the dog to turn in both directions, clock wise and anti-clock wise.

You can introduce the cue words, 'Turn Left and 'Turn Right'.

Build on the exercise slowly, until eventually she no longer needs the hand signal and can turn as soon as she hears the cue.

The final aim is to have the dog standing facing away from you, with her bottom to your legs.

Remember this is not the same as having the dog twist, twirl or spin, where they complete a circle, it is a half-circle to teach your dog to stand with her back to you, or to change direction in the bath or on the grooming table.

The hand that isn't luring her round with the treat, can act as a block, from the dog over turning. Simply keep your hand in place so that when she touches it, she stops turning.

Lots of praise when she is in place, to tell her that is what you want.

The final result is, when your dog is asked to turn, she will turn away from you and stand with her back to you.

Walk Backwards

Why teach walk backwards?

Walking backwards away from you is a great exercise to teach your dog. It serves as many useful purposes.

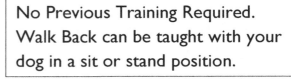

Ace—Top Trick
Walk Back

A Problem Solver
No Previous Training Required. Walk Back can be taught with your dog in a sit or stand position.

It teaches your dog to give you space, to move out of *your* way when you are coming through doorways carrying groceries etc.

It can also *help* with stopping your dog in her track from jumping up.

It also makes your dog become 'back end' aware, as a *dog* generally does not think about what their back feet are doing.

Being back-end aware is a great exercise to teach the show dog, as it helps them in learning how to position their back feet where you want them. Also, a must exercise for anyone considering doing competition obedience.

How to teach Walk Backwards

There are two methods you can try to find out which suits your dog best

Method 1

(1) Have some treats in your closed fist. Hold your hand up to your chest, so that your dog needs to look up to see it.

(2) Shorten your lead and make sure the position of your lead clip is under her chin. (do not pull up on the lead, it should be a relaxed lead, it is purely there as a block to stop the dog from turning rather than staying facing you).

(3) Get your dog's attention by allowing her to sniff the treat hand then take your hand back to your chest while she watches.

(4) Walk towards your dog and if she moves at all to get out of your way, pay her instantly.

With some dogs, you may have to walk right up, until you are almost touching them, before they move, do not bang into them, but slide your foot between their front paws and keep it there, most dogs will swiftly move out of the way. Any effort to move at all, make sure you pay her.

When I teach this in my classes, this is always a great way of showing me the dog's character. Strong, determined characters will sit steady as a rock when the owner walks up to them, even if they touch them they will not move, assertive dogs will often jump up on the owner. Sensitive dogs will leap out of the way as soon as you get too close.

Repeat 5 to 10 times and pay every effort to move, no matter how small, to help her grasp what it is you are asking of her.

Once she starts to move more freely, introduce your cue, my cue is

'Walk Back'. Say 'Walk Back', as she is actually moving, not before she starts.

Dog Trainer's Notes

This exercise is a great way of showing me the character of the dogs in my class.

Strong determined characters will sit steady as a rock when the owner walks up to them, even if they touch them they will not move.

o   Assertive dogs will often jump up on the owner to claim the space if the owner moves in to close.

o   Sensitive dogs will leap out of the way as soon as you get too close.

Owners and dogs love this exercise and this exercise opens so many other doors for other exercises. Really worth teaching this.

Depending on the dog and their reaction to the above method, if the owner and dog seem to be struggling with it, try **Method 2** as an alternative.

Method 2 (An alternative method)

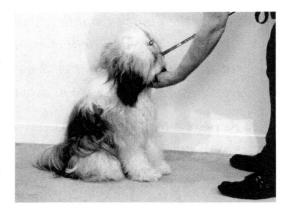

(1) Ask your dog to sit or stand in front of you.

(2) With a treat in your hand, take your hand to your dog and place it under their chin, towards her chest.

To access the treat in your hand, your dog will have to move to reach your hand.

Your dog should move her backend to see the hand with the treat in.

(3) The minute she comes up into a stand mark the behaviour with 'Yes' and reward her.

Repeat until she becomes consistent.

(4) Introduce your cue word 'Walk Back', the moment your dog starts to move her backend.

Head Down

(Chin resting on the floor between paws)

Why Teach Head Down?

Teaching your dog to put her head down and remain still. This a great exercise to help her to calm down and settle, it can also stop her from barking. Did I mention how cute it looks too?

Ace—Top Trick
A Problem Solver

Head Down - It would be helpful if your dog knows how to lie down, before attempting to teach head

Teaching Head Down

Start with your dog lying down, with her tummy touching the floor.

You will do this by sitting on the floor to the side and front of your dog. The hand closest to her acts as a roof or shelter, under which you will teach her to place her head. The other hand (which is furthest away from her) will encourage her under and pay her with the treats.

Place your shelter hand parallel to the ground, in front of your dog's head and close enough to the floor so that she places her chin flat on the floor to get her head under your hand, to reach the treat. Lure her with the treat, to place her head under your hand.

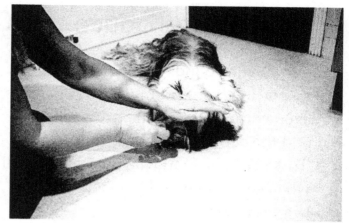

Once under, pay her a few treats in quick succession to encourage her to keep her head there for a few seconds. When you finish paying her, remove your shelter hand and your treat hand and start again.

If she is reluctant to put her head under, lift your shelter hand a bit higher until she gets the idea, and lower it gradually, but make sure you pay her well, to help encourage her.

As your dog gets more comfortable placing her head under your hand and keeping it there, gradually lower the shelter hand to the floor. She will eventually have no option but to touch her chin to the floor to get the treat.

Once she is doing this willingly, spread the payment of the treats out more, increasing the time in which she gets them by 10 seconds increments.

Practice this over 20-30 times until she is happily and confidently, placing her head under your hand.

To check if she understands what you are asking Place your shelter hand out flat but hide the treats. Wait a few seconds to see if she places her head under your hand on her own. If she does, say 'Yes' instantly and quickly start paying her with treats, tell her she is a good girl. If she does not quite get it, then go back to the last step where you lured her.

Time to introduce the Cue Word

Once she responds to the shelter signal, by placing her head under your hand even without seeing the treats, you can add the cue word. My cue for this is 'Head Down'. Remove your hand signal when she does it and pay her while her head is down.

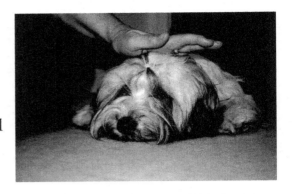

Say the cue before you show the signal, the cue will then tell her what signal is coming and she will start to predict it when she hears the words on cue, by placing her head on the floor.

You can also extend the amount of time she holds that position by waiting progressively longer before paying her with the treats.

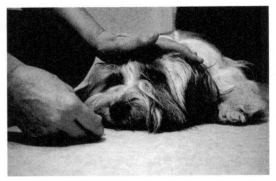

It is time to test how well she knows the 'Head Down' cue. By walking away a few steps, give the cue, 'Head Down' and wait to see if she places her head down, make a huge fuss of her and pay well if she gets it. If not, back up a step or two and keep trying.

Head Up

To teach Head-up, is a very simple step. While your dog's chin is resting on the floor, take a treat to her nose and when she lifts her head from the floor to reach the treat, give the cue 'Head Up', and tell her she's good. Repeat this every time she does head down.

Mr Tibs—Training Tips:

Make sure you don't lose your dog's normal down position and she doesn't start offering the 'Head Down' as soon as you ask for a down.

Only accept the head down if it is what you have asked for.

Quiet Please

The importance of teaching your dog to be quiet

There is nothing worse than living with a constant barker, and it is probably even worse if you are the neighbour next door to a constant barker. To restore quiet to your house it is helpful if you can work out why your dog is barking. Is she barking to tell you someone is approaching? Is she barking because she sees people passing the house while she is looking out the window? Is she barking because she wants attention? Or perhaps she is barking because she is excited. Whatever the reason, it will help if you know why she is doing it. There are a few methods that can help in controlling the level of your dog's barking, but I am going to concentrate on the one method here that I feel can be a fun exercise in the long run to teach. Teaching your dog to bark on command, so that you can teach her to be quiet, are you confused? Read on.

Why would you Teach Bark or Speak on Cue?

Let me explain. I know it probably sounds a little peculiar, to teach your dog to do something that you would rather she did not do, but I promise it makes sense.

Teaching your dog to be quiet on cue, may well prove to be one of your more challenging exercises if your dog's barking habit has been going on a long time. However, it is guaranteed to be one of the most rewarding things you will teach your dog.

For many owners they resolve themselves to the fact that there is no option, but to live with it. It does not have to be that way, but it does rely on some commitment from you and as I said, do not expect to see results overnight.

Making a Difference Instantly

As I mentioned there are many reasons that the dog will bark, the following are some tips to encourage an instant change to your dog's behaviour, without making these modifications, it could mean the difference between your teaching being successful and unsuccessful.

Barking at passers-by

So, your dog barks at people approaching your house, passing by the house, or even at cars parking outside your house. The number one change to make is:

Do Not Allow your dog to look out of windows

As cute as it is to see your dog watching out the window, there is nothing that is more likely to guarantee a barker than this. Looking out windows provides your dog the opportunity for your dog to become territorial. Many dogs will claim their territory, as far as the eye can see which can be quite a distance.

Even watching out the window in to your garden can encourage this behaviour, when the creatures of the night venture into your garden, cats, foxes, badger, rabbits, deer, seeing these animals enter your dog's territory can be enough to justify your dog to wake the whole house up.

During the day, birds or even aeroplanes passing the garden may be enough for some dogs to launch a protest. Unless you can do anything to stop the invaders then the easiest solution is to block your dog's access to every window.

What to do about the door barker

If your dog barks because someone is at the door or entering the house, the number one change to make is:

Do Not allow your dog access to the front door when someone is arriving

This creates an over excitement when people are entering or even a territorial attitude. Often this is triggered by the charge or run to the front or back door when someone knocks. Blocking this to begin with will be a huge advantage and help to calm your dog, providing you with the opportunity to retrain them.

What to do about the garden barker

If your dog barks when she is out in the garden on her own, the number one tip is:

Do not allow unsupervised access to the garden

If you have a dog that is, well exercised, trained and socialised they do not need constant excess to your garden, to charge around. It is your garden and you need to take control of it.

Allowing your dog to, freely roam your garden will create territorial behaviour. Dogs start to pick up, on sounds far and near, i.e. other neighbourhood dogs, people in their gardens etc. All these sounds will be good grounds for your dog to let the neighbourhood know she is there. This behaviour is much easier to bring under control if your dog's garden time is restricted and supervised. Unfortunately, many people do not like the idea of their dog not accessing the garden, as it keeps the dog occupied and she is less trouble for them than when in the house.

In my opinion, this is a lazy way of training and needs addressing as it does not meet the needs of your dog and causes problems that you, your dog and your neighbours, really do not need, including digging, chewing and of course the barking.

What to do about the left-alone barker

If your dog barks when left home alone the number one tip is:

Understanding what is causing her to bark. It is crucial to being able to solve the problem.

Diagnosing what is triggering it.

o Does she bark the minute you leave the house?

o Does she bark after she has been alone for a while?

o Is someone coming to the door and disturbing her?

o Does she bark even if you leave the room?

- It is crucial for curing the behaviour that you understand what is causing it.

Whatever her reason for barking, your dog may be heading into a behaviour, known as Separation Anxiety. It is important to get to the bottom of this, to find the underlying cause and quickly. Understanding what is triggering the anxiety and helping your dog overcome it is essential, as this is very stressful for your dog and they will be very unhappy.

Separation Anxiety shows itself to various degrees in the form of barking, destroying, toileting. It can come in the form of one or more of these behaviours and can escalate overtime, it generally does not go away, and it gets worse if left untreated. This disorder led me to write my first ever small dedicated book, 'It's Okay to Be Alone'; this book will teach you everything you need to know about it, including how to solve it.

http://www.amazon.co.uk/Its-Okay-Alone-separation-anxiety-ebook/dp/B00UEKN760

If your dog is barking because she has developed a habit of being territorial or over excited, then it is your job to teach her to behave in a different manner. For your dog to learn to be quiet when told, she will need to know what it is she is doing. A good way of helping her understand this, is to teach her to bark on command and then reverse it, this is a very good way to start to bring peace and quiet to your home.

If you are one of the lucky ones, who does not have a barker then you might want to omit this exercise, unless you'd like to teach it as a trick.

Just because you teach it as a trick, does not mean you will create a barking dog, as long as you are thorough in your teaching.

Barking on Cue

Arm yourself with a pocket full of treats and, if possible, take your dog to where she is most likely to bark.

As soon as she starts to bark, pay her with a treat. Repeat this, 5 to 10 times. She should quickly become at least a little consistent with the barking now.

Add your cue, I use 'Speak' for barking, but you can use whatever you want.

Every time she barks, say 'Speak' and pay her with the treat.

After 10 repetitions say the word 'Speak' before she barks and wait to see what happens, if she barks or makes any sound reward her by paying her.

You can now work on repeatedly asking her to bark when you tell her.

When she is consistently barking when she hears the word 'Speak', it is time to teach the all-important word, 'Quiet'.

Quiet on Cue

Ask your dog to 'Speak' and when she barks 2 or 3 times, say 'Quiet' and then put a treat in front of her nose. When she stops barking to sniff the treat, praise her and pay her with the treat.

Repeat 5 to 10 times and make sure you pay up instantly when she stops barking.

You now need to test her in different areas and situations but build it up slowly. Have someone knock on your door and practice asking her to be quiet. You will need to put a treat under her nose the first few times until she gets the hang of it.

As your dog becomes more reliable, you can also try adding an 'incompatible behaviour' that can help further to stopping the problem and gives your dog something else to think about.

Mr Tibs—Training Tip

If you are teaching 'Speak' with the intention of teaching your dog to be quiet, then it is important that you no longer reward your dog for barking at this stage, since this is the behaviour that you want to change.

Rewarding quiet moments, when your dog offers them, should be your primary target. Unless you want to keep the barking cue as an exercise/trick.

In this Chapter

o Using an incompatible behaviour as backup
o In your bed
o Food refusal
o Ringing the bell to go outside

Using an incompatible behaviour as a backup

What is an incompatible behaviour?

In the last chapter, we looked at teaching your dog to bark on cue and to be quiet on cue. If your dog is a barker, using another behaviour to make it difficult for your dog to bark, can help create a habit in a short space of time. This would be known as, 'an incompatible behaviour'. For example, you could ask your dog to Lie Down and put her Head Down, which you will have taught her earlier on in the book. It is very difficult for your dog to bark with her head/chin resting on the floor. This is what makes it incompatible with 'Barking', but do not forget to reward and reward well, when your dog is giving you what you want.

Another example of an incompatible behaviour would be, teaching your dog to go to a mat every time the doorbell rings, running and sitting on a mat would prevent your dog from jumping up on visitors or running out your door when it opens.

I hope this helps you in looking out for other incompatible behaviours.

Dog Trainer's Notes

In a class situation, it is a good idea to look for incompatible behaviours that will work for certain dogs in your class, who may be disruptive for others.

For example, the dog who is barking to get to another dog in the class. The 'incompatible behaviour' would be to have the owner to encourage their dog to sit facing them and watch them, at the same time they are presenting their back to the other dog.

In your Bed

Why teach 'In Your Bed'?

Teaching your dog to go to her bed when you ask, will save a whole lot of time when you are in a hurry, this avoids stress and tension, caused through having to try

Ace—Top Trick
A problem solver

No Previous Training Required
o An essential exercise that every dog should learn.
o Never use your dog's bed as a reprimand.

catching her, or get hold of her to put her in her bed. Her bed, whether it is a crate or standard dog bed, should be a place of rest, it should never be used as a punishment.

In the early days of teaching and bonding with your dog, it is important that your dog is not permitted to sleep anywhere other than in her own bed, this means not on your bed, the sofa, the floor or in

multiple dog beds. Only one bed and that is the only place she can occupy until the boundaries are established.

'Go to Bed' is very different to 'Go Mat' and the two should not be confused. When you teach Go Mat, your dog will remain alert and attentive to you, expecting another cue, within a relatively short space of time. Go Mat is great for in the class room as it's a wonderful tool for teaching your dog Distance Control.

'Go to Bed' is a place for your dog to settle down and rest for a while.

When I teach the dog to Go to Bed, I am wanting the dog to relax and settle down when sent to their bed, not waiting on when the next treat is coming or for a release command to allow her to move. However, dogs are creatures of habit and very easily learn to love anything that is associated with good experiences. For many dogs, this will be food and if your dog is not a foody, this is easily learnt, by altering their feeding regime so that they work for their dinner.

Whether you have taught 'Go Mat,' or 'Go to Bed' first, both will complement the other, it should be quick and simple to teach, as they are both taught along the same principle.

What you will need

o   A dog crate or dog bed, tasty treats and your dog of course.

How Long Can My Dog Be Crated?

At night when dogs sleep, their body systems and their need to toilet, slow down. Therefore, they can sleep all night without toileting from a fairly young age. However, just because she may sleep 8 or 10 hours at night does not mean this can happen or should happen in the daytime. In the daytime, your dog will sleep lighter, for shorter periods and will then want to be out of bed investigating, playing, toileting etc.

If a young dog is to be crated for more than two hours, it is best to make water available to them, by attaching a water bottle dispenser to the crate, (or a clip-on bowl attached in the crate, will prevent potential spillages and her bed from getting wet).

The crate must never, be used as a reprimand, or as a place to put your dog because you do not have time to play with them. The following is an approximate guideline for how long a dog from puppyhood to adulthood can be expected to stay in a crate, although they still must be taught to accept this.

4 hours is about the maximum amount of time your dog should spend in a crate, this is a long time being left, in a small area, and all dogs should have provisions made for them to receive a break after this period.

Den Time
A guide to the maximum time your dog should be left in a crate.

Dogs aged:

✓	8 to 10 weeks	30 to 60 minutes
✓	11 to 16 weeks	1 to 2 hours
✓	6 to 18 months	3 hours
✓	2 years +	3 to 4 hours

Times are given as a guide only.
Excessive time spent in a crate could compromise your dog's mental and physical well-being.

If you have a puppy or dog and work all day, it is essential that your dog be given a break from the confines of the crate, after 4 hours. This is for her wellbeing both mentally and physically. Even with a break, 4 hours is still a long time to have to lie in the same spot, so she will still need to be taught to accept this amount of time over many months, even up to 18 months to 2 years. It is essential if you are to leave your dog for this length of time that she

gets a good walk and romp in the morning, before you leave for work, another one during lunch time and again after work. If you are unable to come home at lunchtime to give her this freedom, then **you must** bring in a dog walker to break up her crate time, but this does not and should not replace her time with you. Morning time and after work play and training sessions, are still essential times spent with you.

I am constantly surprised at how many people choose to own a dog during their busy schedules and think that by bringing a dog walker in, equates to giving them time. If 'you' do not spend the time working, playing and bonding with your dog, she will not listen to you, there will be no respect towards you and she will become disconnected from you when out on walks.

Tibetan Terriers, are just one breed who are naturally inclined to be more independent than some other breeds. They will become completely uninterested in you and adapt quickly to making their own decisions and going it alone, without being given quality time from you. This may make living with them difficult and other behavioural issues can develop for breeds such as this.

Crate training is a temporary tool, some dogs love their crate so much they do not want to lose it. They feel safe and secure with a crate as their den, knowing it is their own safe-haven, where they can relax and nothing bad happens.

Your aim however, is to create a dog that can be trusted to have freedom in at least a small part of the house while you are gone, if your circumstances allow it.

It is 'never' a good idea to give your dog complete freedom of the home, this confuses the dog as to what the rules and boundaries are which can lead to further problems down the road. Once your dog can be trusted in the home without toileting or climbing on the work surfaces and stealing from the trash etc., the crate door can be left open, you can keep the crate for her to sleep in, but you can remove the door, or leave the door open. It is also good to keep some continuity with the crate, so that she can still accept times when you may need to close her in, i.e. when you take her on holiday with you, or she needs to stay at someone else's house, or you have work men in the home, this is a good safety measure to implement.

If it is, or was your plan to leave your dog crated daily for an 8-hour day, this will compromise your dog's mental and physical well-being and perhaps you should re-think whether your home is the right home for a dog, you might enjoy it, but will the dog?

Summary

Your dog should receive 45 to 60 mins exercise before being left for a long period in the crate (4 hours).

If she has slept all night in the crate then she must have, 60 to 90 minutes of outdoor exercise in the morning, before being put back in the crate.

Also, in the evening, she must have a good 60 to 90 minutes play/training time, before asking her to settle down at night.

Failure to provide such needs may lead to behaviour problems developing and create a very unhappy and restless dog, which could include barking in the night.

Mr Tibs—Training Tips

✓ To help establish positivity towards the bed, every meal your dog eats should be in her bed.

✓ Treats and chews may also be placed in your dog's bed.

✓ Everything good should be associated with your dog's bed.

✓ It is essential that your dog is encouraged to sleep only in her bed and nowhere else in the home, if problems are to be avoided.

Teaching what 'In Your Bed' means.

My Cue

"In your Bed" or if you prefer, "In your place".

Teaching your dog what the word 'Bed', or 'in your bed' means is very simple.

Each time it is your dog's dinner time take the food bowl to her bed and hold it

over the bed, as soon as she enters the bed give the cue "In Your Bed" and place the bowl in the bed with her.

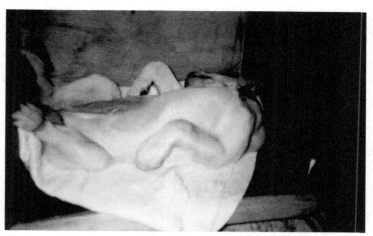

Repeat this step with every meal and every treat. Take the treat to the bed, hover your hand over the bed and wait, when she enters the bed say, 'In Your Bed' and feed.

You will quickly find that as you start towards the bed the dog starts to race you to it. When this happens, start saying, 'In your bed', as she is going towards it. When she reaches the bed, say 'Yes', to mark the behaviour and then give her the food.

As she gets more consistent at this step, you will want to test if she understands the cue.

Pick up her dinner or treats, turn to her and say, 'In your bed', and watch for what result you get. If she runs straight to her bed say, 'Yes' and go to her and feed her.

Now you can test her by looking at her without the treat in your hand and saying, 'In your Bed', and see what happens. If she does not go, help her, do not leave her to become frustrated. Do a few more runs of the previous steps until it becomes clearer to her.

If she heads straight to her bed, mark the behaviour with an excited 'Yes' and jackpot her with a few extra treats.

You now need to increase the time she waits in the bed. I find initially if you jackpot her with a few consecutive extra treats, the more treats she gets in one hit, the more likely she is to stay in the position. The aim is to wean her off the treats, with the occasional random treat being sufficient.

For more comprehensive details on crate/den training please see my other books 'Pre-Vaccination Puppy Training' and 'It's Okay to be Alone'.

Food Refusal

Why teach food refusal?

Food refusal can keep your dog safe from picking up and eating what could be harmful to her when out on a walk. Food refusal also makes hand-feeding your dog easier as they learn to control how they take the food from you.

Ace—Top Trick

A Problem Solver

No previous training needed
✓ What you need – A pouch full of treats and your dog.
✓ This exercise is best taught down at your dog's level. Kneel on the floor in front of her.

Teaching food refusal in three stages.

Stage 1 –   learning to leave the closed hand which is full of food.

Stage 2 –   learning to ignore food she can see in your open hand.

Stage 3 –   learning to leave what is on the floor.

Stage 1

Learning not to touch the closed hand which is full of food.

(1) Take a fistful of small treats, extend your hand to your dog and allow her to sniff and work at your hand. Young dogs may get over excited at this stage and try to bite on your hand, if this happens, remove your hand momentarily and then try again until she calms down, she will eventually calm down, if you are patient with her.

How determined the dog is to get the food is governed by the individual dog and how greedy or desperate they are to get that food. Keep your hand very still and wait.

(2) At the first moment she stops, touching your hand, even for a second, feed her instantly.

Repeat Step 1. She will very quickly work out that if she does not touch your hand she gets fed. Your timing in releasing the reward to her is extremely important, as this is what will tell her what it is you want.

Once she gets the idea, the aim is for you to bring your hand down to her, and for her not to touch it at all. This will take a lot of self-control on her part, make sure you pay well when she gets it right.

Once she has reached this stage, it is time to try Stage 2.

Stage 2

Learning to ignore food she can see in your open hand.

(1) Extend your fist to your dog with food in.

(2) When the dog is not touching your hand, open your hand, palm up, so that she can see the food.

If she moves towards your hand, even slightly, close your hand around the food instantly. Wait until she has settled again and repeat the process.

It is important that you do not pull your hand back, or away from her. Keep your hand perfectly still and simply close your hand if she attempts to approach it.

Try to perfect your reflexes so that you are quicker than she is, she must not get to steal the food, or this will take longer to teach.

If she is very determined and enthusiastic to take the food, keep your hand further away, to give you a chance to win at the game, until she understands what you want, and then gradually bring your hand closer to her.

The aim of this exercise is for you to have an extended hand open with food on your palm and her not to touch it unless you offer it to her. Once she has mastered this and is very clear that she is not to touch what has not been given to her, it is time to teach her Stage 3, 'Leave what is on the floor'.

Stage 3

Learning to leave what is on the floor

Have some food in your hand and place your hand palm side down on the floor, so that the food is under it and hidden from sight. Your dog may lie down when you do this, as she may see it as a down signal, or simply because it puts her closer to getting the treat.

Pretty much the same as showing her the food in your hand, in Stage 2, show her the food on the floor, by lifting your hand off it, if she attempts to approach it, hide it again, wait until she settles and try again.

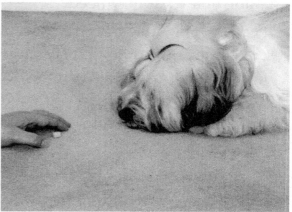

If she starts digging to access the food, stand your ground and do not let her get it. She will eventually leave it.

If she leaves it even for a second, when she has seen it, release a piece of food to her to mark the behaviour you want.

Repeat these steps in quick succession until she waits for longer whilst looking at the food.

Once she is leaving it consistently, you can add a cue to it. As you lift your hand and she remains sitting, cue her with the word 'Off' or 'Leave'.

Ringing a Bell for toilet breaks

Why teach your dog to ring a bell?

Teaching your dog to ring a bell to go outside is a fun way of having your dog communicate with you and telling you what they need.

> ## Ace—Top Trick
> **A Problem Solver**
> No previous training needed
> You will need a bell of some description, preferably one that you can hang by the door and your dog can reach.

It can be preferable than having a dog who barks at the door, scratching at the door or just standing there in the hope that you will notice she is cross-legged and in desperate need of a toilet break. It is much easier to teach than you would imagine and rewarding for you the owner, knowing your dog can tell you and no longer has accidents on the floor.

What you will need: A bell or bells of some description. The bells I use are children's wrist sleigh bells which can be hung on a lead. I should have marketed these years ago as I have been teaching this for so long I can't remember, of course someone else has marketed the idea, so if you desire you can buy Dog doorbells online if you do a search.

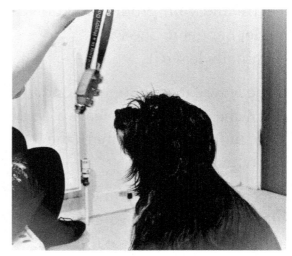

Step 1

The first step is to hold the bell close to your dog's nose. Once your dog sniffs or touches the bell, say "Yes!" and give her a treat. If needed, you can encourage your dog to touch the bell by holding a treat behind it or dabbing some peanut butter on the bell, although be careful of adding tasty scent to the object as it may encourage the dog to grab at it or want to chew on it, this would not be a good idea, so only resort to this as an absolute last resort.

Step 2

Repeat Step 1, until she readily touches the bell with her nose, always giving lots of praise and a treat. When she confidently touches the bell as soon as you present it, add a word "Bell." Start to hold the bell a little farther away, to encourage her totake one or two steps towards it, to touch it.

Step 3

Once she has learnt to touch the bell on cue, in your hand, hang the bell from the doorknob on the door where you would like her to go out to toilet. Encourage her to touch the bell, by keeping your hand on the bell as a contact point. (Note, if you remove yourself from the object too soon, the chances are your dog won't have a clue, as the success up to now,

will have been all about you and the object). As soon as she takes any step towards the bell, say "Yes!" and treat with lots of praise.

Step 4

Repeat until she readily touches the bell when you give her the cue. Reward her and go wild with enthusiastic praise, this is a big deal and she needs to know it and know that this is what you want.

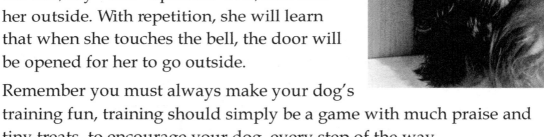

Step 5

Step 5 is teaching her to ring the bell at the right time. Approach the door with your dog, point to the bell, and give your cue, "Bell." Or 'Ring the Bell'. The moment she touches the bell, say "Yes!" open the door, and take her outside. With repetition, she will learn that when she touches the bell, the door will be opened for her to go outside.

Remember you must always make your dog's training fun, training should simply be a game with much praise and tiny treats, to encourage your dog, every step of the way.

Everyone in your household should follow the same training method and use the same cues, to avoid confusing your dog.

Remember, dogs have a short attention span in the early days of training, so have **brief training sessions** several times a day. When you know she has caught on to what you want, you can give her a jackpot of several tiny treats, one right after another, to encourage her to repeat the task.

Mr Tibs—Training Tips

✓ If your dog begins to ring the bell just to go outside to play (it happens occasionally with some dogs) you need to teach her that ringing the bell is only about toilet time.

✓ Next time she rings the bell, clip on her leash, and take her to the place where you want her to go. Give her a few minutes and if she does her business, give her lots of praise and in this instance, I would even give a treat.

✓ If, however she doesn't go, take her straight back inside and wait until she asks again.

✓ You must always respond to your dog when she rings the bell, if it is to remain consistent and reliable, to ignore it could lead to causing your dog to fail.

NOTES

In this Chapter

o What is 'Go Mat'

o Why teach Go Mat?

o Teaching Go Mat'?

o Increasing your dog's time on the mat

o Moving the mat to other rooms or outdoors

What is Go Mat?

For many years, I have taught this exercise and it has become a signature for my classes, every dog that ever trained with me, will

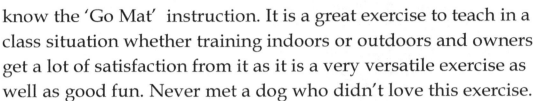

Ace—Top Trick
A problem-solver

No previous training is required

know the 'Go Mat' instruction. It is a great exercise to teach in a class situation whether training indoors or outdoors and owners get a lot of satisfaction from it as it is a very versatile exercise as well as good fun. Never met a dog who didn't love this exercise.

It is a fantastic exercise for teaching to young puppy's, who learn it in super quick time and they delight in knowing where you want them to be and what they are meant to do, which is why 'Go Mat' matters so much.

Every dog can learn to 'Go Mat' in a relatively short space of time, there are no age restrictions and there is nothing difficult about it. To have your dog go to a mat when told is useful for many reasons.

Why Teach Go Mat?

- It gives your dog a focal point.

- It is a great tool for teaching your dog to be calm when needed, preventing her from making mistakes.

- It is a great exercise for when visitors arrive, when someone's at your door or you are eating.

- In addition, a great exercise to have fun with outdoors.

- As a trainer, this is a wonderful addition to class training.

- It is a wonderful exercise to practice shaping behaviour with.

Shaping behaviours is where we wait for the dog to offer what we are looking for and then we mark the behaviour with a 'clicker' or 'yes' word, to indicate they have done what you want and then reward. There is no need for luring (although you can switch to luring if you are impatient and do not want to wait). To shape a behaviour, you simply stay quiet and watch for the dog to offer what we want. i.e. Your dog moves towards the mat, you mark this action with the 'Yes' word and reward with a treat. You gradually hold back on marking the behaviour until the dog puts her feet on it, sits on it or downs on it, whichever is your preferred position to begin with.

As a rule, I send the dog to the mat and ask for a Down, but your dog needs to know a Down away from the mat, before you can ask for it on the mat.

What you will need

Pick a suitable mat, a small bath mat or doormat, preferably with non-slip backing, and some tasty treats.

Cue Words - 'Go Mat' you can use something different, like 'Go Mark', 'Place' etc. but be sure it is different to 'bed' This exercise should not be confused with 'Go to Bed'. The release cue is 'Okay', unless you have a preferred word.

Teaching Go Mat

Shaping the required behaviour

(1) Start by standing close to and facing the mat, with your dog beside you.

Say nothing but wait and watch. If your dog investigates the mat at all, say 'Yes' and reward her straight away.

Be patient and keep rewarding for any interest in the mat. You are looking for her to make contact with the mat. If she puts a paw on the mat, say 'Yes' and reward every time. You are going to build this up until she puts two paws then 3 paws then 4 onto the mat, (assuming she fits onto the mat you have chosen of course, otherwise tailor your training accordingly).

Having the mat right in front of you makes it easier for her to accidentally target and gives you opportunity to reward her.

(2) As soon as 'all four feet' are on the mat, say 'Yes', praise and throw the reward for her, straight away.

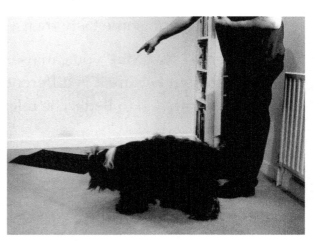

(3) Repeat this several times. Most dogs will go to the mat on cue after a few short repetitions.

To test whether your dog has made the connection that you are looking for, move just a step or two away from the mat and wait to see if she goes to the mat. If she gets it even with one paw a huge enthusiastic 'Yes' and toss the reward.

If she is showing signs of understanding that you want her on the mat, it is time to introduce the cue word. As she makes contact with the target (the mat), give the cue, 'Go Mat'.

Build up her distance from the mat, one-step at a time.

Mr Tibs—Training Tip

Throwing the food reward away from the mat, allows the dog the opportunity to go away from the mat and repeatedly come back to the mat, otherwise they will stay on the mat and this is then harder to reward. Depending of course what you are wanting your dog to do.

(4) Start to watch for her heading towards the mat and bring the timing of your cue forward. i.e. as she is heading towards the mat, say 'Go Mat' followed by 'Yes', when she connects with the mat.

(5) You now need to delay your 'Yes' by a few seconds, so that she learns to stay there for longer, increase the time gradually.

(6) Once she is staying put, waiting for her 'Yes' marker, it is time to introduce the release command. We want her to learn that staying on the mat is what you want, until she hears 'Okay', this is the release command for every exercise.

Adding the Down

(7) Once your dog is putting all four feet on the mat, when you give the word, you can ask her to lie down if she already knows this or wait until she offers the behaviour and mark it.

(8) Give her the cue "Go Mat" and as soon as she gets to her mat, give the cue "Down." It may take her a few minutes to get it the first few times, but after a few practice sessions, she should lie down automatically when she gets to the mat after you give her the "Go Mat" cue.

Once she has done this several times, she should only be getting treats and praise when she lies down on the mat when told to "Go Mat".

Increase the length of time

(9) Now that your dog is consistently lying down on her mat after you give her the "Go mat" cue, you can increase the amount of time she spends on her mat.

To do this, slowly add a few seconds before she gets the treat after she responds to the cue. Slowly add small increments of time between the time your dog responds correctly to the cue and the time she gets a treat.

If your dog makes a mistake and gets up from her mat before you give her the treat, simply give her the "Go Mat" cue again and go back to the last point where your dog was successful.

By slowly adding to the amount of time your dog stays on the mat, you will soon be able to give her the cue and have her stay in her place while you have dinner or invite a visitor in until they are settled, then she can be allowed to greet them

Mr Tibs—Training Tip

The mat is not a place to leave your dog for long periods of time.

The mat is a target to keep your dog focused and out of the way when she could be a hazard, for short periods of time i.e. stopping her jumping up when visitors arrive or stopping her running out the door when you need to answer it.

o Send her to her bed, if you are going to expect her to stay out of the way for longer.

o It is very important when you give your dog the treat that you place the treat on the mat or throw it to the mat.

o Do not feed her from your hand, as this will encourage the dog to follow your hand off the mat.

o If you have an enthusiastic or impatient dog that jumps off the mat as soon as she has had her treat, you need to teach her that it is in her best interests to stay on it longer, by following these steps.

Increasing your dog's time on the mat continued

Once your dog is on the mat, come down to her level, this will encourage her to stay where she is.

Have a collection of small treats in your hand; you are going to feed her consecutively approximately 10 times, while she remains in the down. I cannot stress enough how important it is that the treat is placed or dropped onto the mat, 'NOT' fed from your hand, if your aim is to have her settle on the mat.

If your dog gets up before you have finished feeding her or before you have given her a release cue, simply lure her back to where you want her and finish.

Do not forget to give the release cue; the release cue should be something like, 'OK', or 'That'll do'.

Move to other rooms

If you want to be able to use the "Go Mat" cue in other rooms, or when you are out, wait until your dog has mastered it in one place. Once she understands this, take the mat into another room or area and start the process again. You can also take one or two mats outside in your garden or park and practice it with more distractions until she learns to stay focused on you.

Not all dogs transfer what they learn to different areas, although some may catch on quickly, and will immediately go to their mat and lie down when you give the cue in a new area. If your dog does not seem to understand that when you take the mat to another room and she hears the cue "Go Mat" she should go to it, you will need to re-teach the exercise in the new room, following the same steps as before. Start from the beginning by giving the cue and luring her over to her mat etc. until she makes the connection that it is the same as before. It should only take a couple of repetitions for her to catch on.

Most dogs learn this command relatively quickly. With just a few short training sessions, you should have a dog who finds the mat on cue.

As a training exercise, you can have a lot of fun with 'Go Mat' as it can also be used to teach your dog to give you all her other cues from a distance.

As I said before, in no way should the mat be used to send your dog to it for long periods of time, or your dog will start to dislike the mat. The mat should be used as a temporary position for your dog to wait until she hears another cue from you or the release cue, 'Ok', that tells her the exercise is over.

Once your dog understands to go to the mat and wait for another cue, you can start asking your dog to give you all the other exercises she knows, i.e. Sit, Stand, Sit High etc.

Dog Trainer's Notes

o One of the best exercises to teach in any class situation. You will wonder what you ever did before having this exercise in your class.

o It won't take long before owners are remarking how useful this exercise is in their home.

o Encourage each owner to bring their own mat with them, dog's much prefer a mat they know, they love to know what's theirs, and where they are meant to be.

o All the positions you teach in class, Sit, Down, Stand, Flat, Over etc:

o Should all be taught on the mat, once the dog has learnt them with the owner. This will be the beginnings of the dog working from a distance.

In this Chapter

o What is a Recall and Why teach a Recall?
o How to play 'Doggy in the Middle'
o Line training
o Whistle training

What is a Recall and why do we teach a Recall?

The recall is probably one of the most important exercises for your dog to learn. The recall keeps your dog safe, the Recall saves time, and the Recall shows respect and a relationship between you and your dog. The Recall is being able to call your dog to you and have her respond immediately.

Many times, I am contacted by owners saying, 'My dog won't come when I call her'. My response is, 'Have you taught her to come when called?' To which there is usually a silence or a blank expression. You see, often we assume that our dogs should know they are supposed to come when we call them, but how can they know this, if it has never been taught? Your dog can only be guilty of not doing what she is told, if she was taught it in the first place.

It is a good idea to allow your dog her freedom with a long line attached, until she has become responsive to her name and the cue 'Come'. Returning to you when called needs to be developed into a habit. The line will prevent bad habits from happening and help encourage the new habit you want to develop.

To start the teaching process, we are going to use a game called 'Doggy in the Middle' this is a fun game to help your dog grasp the idea or responding as soon as she hears her name.

There are two parts to a Recall. 1. What happens when your dog hears her name and 2. The journey needed to get to you.

Part 1. For me this is the hardest part of the Recall, getting your dog to respond to you by looking at you when she hears her name. When you achieve this first step you are 80% towards getting your dog to come to you. If they don't or won't stop and look at you, the chances are they are not going to come.

How to play 'Doggy in the Middle'

You need at least two people to play this game, the purpose of the game is get your dog to run happily between two people when she hears her name and the cue 'Come'.

Step 1. Start in one room of your house, with 2 people, both should have 5 to 10 small treats, no bigger than your little finger nail, each person in turn calls the dog to them, following these steps.

Cue – Dog's name first, this should get her attention and she will turn and look at you.

Hold your hand out with the treat in it, encouraging her to come to you.

As she starts moving towards you, introduce the word 'Come' in an exciting tone, encouraging her all the way to you.

When she reaches you, mark the behaviour with 'Yes' and reward her with the treat to reinforce it. DO NOT ask her to sit at this stage, for three reasons:

A. This would slow down her coming to you, as she anticipates having to do a Sit.

B. It makes the game boring for the dog if she is asked to sit each time she comes to you.

C. She will enjoy it much more if she gets to run to you at speed and the reward she receives should be for coming to you, not for sitting. If you want her to learn to sit when she reaches you, reward her first for coming, then ask for a sit and reward the sit, this way she gets two rewards.

Take her to different rooms in the house and practice the same exercise, perhaps the living room, the kitchen and the hall.

You can gradually add a third or fourth person to the game once she begins to understand how to play.

Alternatively, you can alternate which two people get to play the game.

This is a great game for the children to get involved with, but you must keep control of it so that she doesn't get confused and give up.

Remember dogs tire quickly when learning something new, so play must stop once all the food is gone.

Step 1 should be played two or three times a day for 1 week, before you move on to step 2.

Step 2. Now your dog is recalling instantly between the two of you, increase the distance, perhaps have her come from room to room, increase the distance slowly and perhaps start by peeping round the door, so that she knows where you are, if she seems to be struggling. Be patient and help her if she can't work it out. Her desire to find you and get her reward will soon spur her on. Practice calling her into different rooms.

Puppies and dogs lose interest very quickly and it won't take long for her to not see the point of the game if this happens.

Your dog's Recall indoors, should be flawless before moving on to the next stage, Recalling Outdoors, spend an extra week working on Step 2, if there is any doubt about your dog's response.

Mr Tibs—Training Tip

If there are more than two people in your family, your dog should by now be quite proficient at galloping back and forwards when called between the two of you, and It is time to move to the next step.

NOTE: Never call her and 'not' reward her with a treat if you want a reliable Recall.

Recalling Outdoors

Now that your dog can Recall through the house, from room to room without seeing who is calling her, you can practice the same exercise in the garden, where the distractions are much greater.

Remember

You have the sights, sounds and smells of the garden to compete with.

You must make yourself more interesting and exciting than the world around her.

Step 1. You are going to practice this in the garden to teach her that she should respond the same way in every environment. Practice every day at least twice a day for 1 week.

Step 2. You can then practice recalling her from the garden, back into the house. Make sure someone can see her at all times if you go back into the house to call her just in case she doesn't respond to you. You must return to the garden instantly and help her to regain her focus on you.

Step 3. Once your dog has achieved Step 2 and is 100% reliable from the garden, you can then begin to teach 'Doggy in the Middle' in your local park.

You will need to go back to Step 1 again and practice calling her from person to person to remind her what it is she is meant to do.

I would highly recommend that you use a long, flat training line in the park for safety reasons, until she is responding reliably outside, remember old habits die hard and she may regress to what she use to do outside. *(See 'Lifeline Training', for more details of how to do this. Next page).*

The line also allows you to guide or block any behaviour if she is getting it wrong.

Mr Tibs — Training Tip

Practice Step 2. For at least 1 or 2 weeks, before progressing to Step 3.

Full Lifeline Training

I have given quite a bit of space to this section, I really do believe that this exercise will offer the lifeline, that many, many people will need. This exercise allows your dog the freedom to run, explore and meet new friends, but provides a safety mechanism and learning opportunity that you will find invaluable. Without even trying, the lifeline shapes a behaviour that teaches your dog to stay within a certain distance and being by you is the best place to be.

What is a lifeline?

A lifeline is a very long lead, which allows you the opportunity to let your dog exercise, while at the same time keeping her safe until she understands the Recall.

Lifeline training is also an excellent method of retraining a dog who has learnt the art of avoiding being caught when it's time to go back onto the lead, or for reshaping the behaviour of not coming when called.

Ace—Top Trick
A Problem Solver

Lifeline training gives you extra confidence, until your dog starts to respond. A dog won't naturally transfer what they have learnt indoors to the outdoors. You will need to teach her that each game applies in all situations. She will however learn it faster as she already understands it.

Since I began working with a lifeline some 20 years ago, when I would make my own, there are now many types available to buy, they are called training lines or tracking lines. Having worked with a few of them and I find the Mikki training line my preferred choice, due to it being lightweight and flat, this makes it less likely to tangle. They cost around £8 or £9 and can be purchased online by typing Mikki training line into *Google*. You may also find them in good pet stores.

Benefits of Lifeline training

1. The Lifeline allows you the security of knowing that your dog can have freedom to run and play without getting into trouble until she learns good behaviour.

2. A Lifeline prevents your dog from developing unwanted behaviour i.e. running away with objects she has stolen or running away in the park and getting into danger, hence the name Lifeline.

3. A Lifeline lets you communicate with your dog from a distance, without getting into confrontational situations.

4. A Lifeline helps to communicate to your dog that wherever she is and whatever she is doing you are still her leader and she must respond to what you say.

A Common Question

How long will it take to teach my dog to come when called?

With a puppy, I use the lifeline for the first approximately 7 months of the dog's life, to condition the behaviour I want and to prevent unwanted behaviours from developing. This is foolproof, and I have never had a recall problem having used this method.

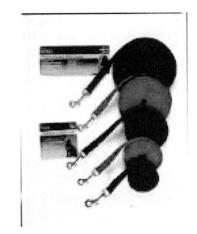

With a dog that has learnt the art of running away, or not coming when called, it depends upon a) the individual dog and b) the work and commitment you put in to breaking the habit your dog has developed, but I approximate 10 to 12 weeks to shape the behaviour you want.

Making your own Lifeline

If you decide to make your own lifeline, it can be made from strong string or cord (Yachting line is best). I find a minimum of 20 to 30 ft. best, the longer the length you are able to handle, the better for your dog. This allows you to control your dog's movements from a greater distance, giving a better long-term result.

How to make a Lifeline

Buy some lightweight Yachting line (20 to 30 ft.) and a trigger hook i.e. lead clasp. Some hardware stores sell both, such as B&Q.

Secure one end of the line to the trigger hook, learn to do a secure knot and it may be best to heat the end of the rope to secure it or tape it. Make sure it is secure or you could have a run-away dog to deal with.

Using the Lifeline Outdoors

Weeks 1 to 4

The line is the ideal solution to teaching your dog to listen to you, when you are in the park, and not to run away.

Weeks 1 to 4 – Personally I like to work with a 30ft line for outdoors, this allows me to give the dog a significant amount of freedom, giving her the feeling of being free which will allow her to act naturally, giving you the opportunity to teach her to respond from a distance.

At this early stage keep hold of the line, at first you will find it awkward due to the length of line, but given time you will get used to it, so don't give up too soon.

You will find the line easier to control if you allow the excess of the line to trail along the ground rather than trying to hold it all, this will also prevent it from getting knotted.

If the dog runs ahead let the line run through your hand or if she goes around a tree, let go of the line and pick it up on the other side.

Don't let the dog go further away than the length of the line.

At different intervals call your dog and firmly but pleasantly insist that she 'Come', reeling her in if necessary, as she gets near hold out a treat and encourage her to you.

Reward her instantly when she reaches you and send her away again with a cue such as 'Go Play'.

As your dog moves away from you, occasionally practice stopping her, by stepping on the line or putting a block on the line by putting tension on it, to stop her from moving forward, at the same time asking her to wait or stop, do not necessarily call her back to you as she will get bored with this. Simply tell her she's good if she stops and then tell her to go play.

Your dog will eventually come to you without you needing to use the line. Practice makes perfect.

Mr Tibs — Training Tip

✓ Half the success of getting your dog back to you is in getting her to stop when you ask her.

✓ If your dog will stop and wait and even look at you, you are half way to getting her to return to you. This is why teaching her to stop and wait is so important.

✓ You can occasionally call your dog to you, but make sure you 'always' offer her a treat for returning to you.

By now if you have put the time in and timed it accurately your dog should be responding as soon as she hears her name. The next stage is:

As soon as your dog starts to return in your direction, tell her she's good, as she is coming to you, so that she knows that you are pleased with her behaviour and that this is what you want. The praise should always be happening as she is coming towards you, continue praising until she arrives at your feet.

When she gets to you take hold of her collar and then give her the treat. The reason for taking hold of the collar is to prevent your dog from learning that touching the collar means her lead is going back on. Many dogs learn from their owners that the minute their hand comes out towards them they should get out of the way as their fun is about to end. This is because the only time the collar is touched is when the lead is going to be put back on, which means she is going back home.

The best reward you can give your dog for coming to you is whatever she was doing at the time you called her i.e. running, playing and sniffing—that's why it is important to call her regularly when out walking and then let her go play again. This will help her realise that calling her doesn't mean the end of fun, not only does she get to go play again she also gets a food reward and lots of praise from you.

Depending upon how often you practiced the exercise of walking your dog, will depend upon whether it is time for you to move onto the next stage. You will have to be the judge of that, if your dog still isn't responding 'reliably', spend longer working on this step, before moving on.

Week 5. Letting go of the line

Your dog has had 4 weeks of learning to only go the distance you allow her on the line, stopping and starting on cue and recalling back to you on cue, these 4 weeks will have been enough time to condition some new responses. It's now time to try letting go of the line, allow her to drag the line behind her wherever she goes.

(1) Practice the very same exercises you worked on in these last 4 weeks, without holding the line.   Asking her to stop on cue and recalling her back to you etc.

(2) When you first start to let go of the line, go to an open or clear area like a field, rather than woodland, this way you can see what's coming and your dog is less likely to get tangled round objects like trees, you can also see your dog clearly and anticipate her next move.

(3) When you first let her go to run, do not call her while she is letting off steam at full speed, you are certain to fail at getting her back, wait until she has drained some of her energy then call her.

(4) You need to alternate on your walks between sometimes holding the line and other times letting go. So that you keep continuity and don't let her go too far from you.

This process of learning to free-run with the line attached is going to take approximately another 5 to 10 weeks. Ensuring she responds to you, every time you call her.

(5) Periodically pick up the line or step on the line, to remind her that she must still respond every time you call her or cue her.

1. Remember to call her back frequently, reward her and let her go again.

2. Don't forget to take hold of her collar before rewarding her.

3. If she decides to run off, you can easily step on the line to stop her.

4. Your dog should be reliable at waiting as soon as she hears the command 'Wait' or 'Stop' now, if you have done your homework.

5. Tie some knots in the line, at different intervals, to enable you to stand on the line without it slipping through under your foot, on the grass.

6. After a time, you will have shaped her behaviour so that the line clipped to her collar means, she must come to you when she hears her name.

7. This exercise may take quite a while to achieve, but do not try to rush things, the longer you take to teach this stage successfully, the more reliable your outcome will be.

Week 10 Decreasing the length of your line

Once you have reached the stage where your dog returns immediately to you upon calling her name and stops when told to wait, it is time to start shortening the line.

🐾 You can either buy a shorter line and test your dog's reactions with this, or snip about a foot off the line, each time you go out to the park. Gradually work down to about six inches, how long it takes to reach this length depends entirely upon how well your dog is responding to you.

🐾 If your dog is not reliable with certain areas of the exercises, Do Not hurry to make the line shorter. Your dog must behave in all situations before moving to each stage.

🐾 You will, in the end be left with just the clip, however do not be in a hurry to dispense with the clip, this could take some time, as your dog will still associate the clip with returning to you.

The lifeline system has been tried and tested repeatedly with great success, if you are having problems with the system, revise your stages and make sure you are not trying to rush things. The longer you keep the line on the more reliable your dog will be.

Dogs are creatures of habit and will become conditioned to staying close to you. I have never failed in teaching a dog to come when called by using this method, I wish you well in your success of having a dog who is a joy to take out and response to working with you and not against you.

Other Uses for the Lifeline include using the Lifeline indoors

The Lifeline has many other uses. I go into homes to visit dogs that are showing signs of possessiveness over objects, people or areas in the home. The benefits of the indoor line are:

1. It allows you to remove your dog from situations and take possession or areas or items, without being confrontational and risking someone being bitten. Your in-house line does not need to be as long as, the outdoor training line. Double lead length will usually do, i.e. about 6ft. You can also by a line this length or again make one. They are called 'Indoor puppy training lines' and can be found at the Company of Animals website. **http://companyofanimals.co.uk/product/clix-puppy-house-line**

2. Jumping on the furniture and refusing to get off.

3. Won't move from her bed when you need her to.

4. Won't come out from under the table or bed when called.

5. Stealing objects and keeping possession of them.

6. Jumping up on visitors

The indoor training line is an ideal tool to help block and retrain these behaviours without confrontation and mishandling of the situation.

Applying the Lifeline in the home

1. Every time you are at home with your dog, ensure the line is attached to her collar. (Never leave your dog alone with the Line ON, she could get caught up on something and get into serious trouble).

The line will become part of her during her time of learning or rehabilitating.

2. Allow your dog to drag the line around behind her, **do not keep hold of it.** Completely ignore the line unless the dog is doing something she shouldn't be.

When do I use it?

3. If your dog jumps on the couch or bed, do not approach the dog, simply pick up the slack of the line and encourage your dog to get off the couch, by using the line.

4. As your dog exits the couch or bed say 'Off', this is your new cue for getting your dog to move away or to move back from anything you don't want her to touch. Praise your dog when she displays the desired behaviour, i.e. jumps off the couch.

5. If she steals socks, or any other item you would rather she didn't have, do not chase after her, pick up the line and encourage her to bring her find to you, reward her with a treat or exchange the item for another toy.

Do not worry that in rewarding her she is going to steal as she thinks she gets rewarded for it, she will not make that connection. She will simply think that giving you what's in her mouth brings about reward, this can only be a good thing.

Mr Tibs — Training Tip

Never leave your dog unsupervised with the line attached.

Controlling your dog's behaviour when you have visitors, using the Lifeline

When visitors call at your house, use the line to address your dog's behaviour at the front door.

1. Announce to your visitor that you will be with them in a moment, while you take charge of your dog, before opening the door.

2. Take hold of the line and ask your dog to Sit, or Go Mat (if you've taught it) before opening the door to your visitor. Insist that she remains sitting the whole time you address your visitor.

3. People will respect that you are trying to control your dog's behaviour and be patient with you. This is preferable to your dog leaping all over them.

4. If your visitor is entering your home, ask them to enter and to go on through to the designated room, while you ensure your dog follows through with your request.

5. As your visitor passes through the house, your dog should remain calm and follow the visitor by sniffing the air as they pass to check them out.

If she gets excited, simply keep calm and calm her down by keeping her in a sit until she settles.

6. Take her through to the room only when she has calmed down and insist that she stays calm by controlling her with your line.

7. Do not allow her to approach the visitor until she is completely calm and relaxed.

This can take quite a while depending upon the dog and how intense her bad habit has become.

Mr Tibs—Training Tip

o It is a very good idea to practice opening and closing your front door while keeping your dog in a sit, without letting her go through it and when there is no one at the door, this will help in developing a habit of not rushing through doors. This will make it easier when people do come to call.

o You should also practice this behaviour with every door in your house, if you show her consistency with regards to entering through all doors, she will get it much faster.

o The Go Mat exercise will also help a lot with this exercise.

Your Cue Words for Lifeline Training

Outdoor Training: 'Come' — this cue is used as your dog is coming towards you, to help her build up the association with the action of returning to you.

'Wait' or 'Stop' — this cue is used when your dog is ahead of you so that you can stop her in her tracks to catch up with her, or so that you can give her further instructions, depending upon the situation.

Indoor Training: 'Off' — this cue is used in the home where we want the dog to move off the furniture, leave an object that's in her mouth or to not put her paws on items like work surfaces etc.

Please Note a FLEXI LEAD or an EXTENDING LEAD is not suitable for dog training and in particular for Line Training.

11 Whistle Training

In this Chapter

o About whistle training
o How to whistle train your dog or puppy

About Whistle Training

Whistle training has been around for many, many years. It is used mostly for training gundogs, although it is also widely used by the Guide Dogs for the Blind Association. The reason both categories use it, is to signal the dog from a distance. The whistle cuts through everything outdoors, which is why it is so important.

Ace—Top Trick

No previous training required

What you need:

- 🖎 A dog
- 🖎 Food
- 🖎 A Whistle

When the gun dog has left the handler, and is running through fields, it is important that she stops when the handler whistles her, so that the handler can give her further instructions on which way to go.

With guide dogs or seeing eye dogs, when they are having free time to run in the park, their owner will not be able to see where they are, the whistle keeps them connected to each other, the dog is trained to return to the owner as soon as they hear the whistle.

For my personal use of the whistle – I train each of my litters to Recall to me when they hear the whistle. This is one of my gifts in my puppy package to the puppy's new owners, as the puppies are well on their way to being recall trained and each will go to their new owner with their own whistle. As long as the new owners follow through with keeping up the training, there should be no problem ever getting their dog back to them, which believe me can be an absolute gift in time saving, when living with a breed like the Tibetan Terrier.

My whistle of choice is the **Acme 210.5** (these are readily available on the internet) This is the whistle I was given to use, when I trained the

Guide Dog puppies, so I have stuck with the same one as I find the pitch of this one perfect, but you can use the whistle of your choice.

How to whistle train your dog or puppy

Whistle training is more conditioning than training and is very easy to teach. All dogs eat, so what we need is the whistle and food. In no time at all your dog will be returning to you at full speed for her food or treat, every time she hears the whistle.

Start by using the whistle every time it's dinner time.

1. Prepare your dog's dinner

2. Hold the bowl of food

3. Have your whistle ready

4. Your dog does not need to be away from you at this stage. No doubt she is sitting watching you prepare her food.

5. While she is watching you, blow the whistle (decide what you want the sound to be beforehand, 1 or 2 pips etc). Your dog will identify this as her Recall signal and give the dog the food straight away.

6. Complete these steps at every meal time for 1 week.

7. Use the same whistle tone for handing her treats as well as her dinner now.

8. After 2 weeks, you can start testing her. When your dog is wandering around the house, give a blow on the whistle and watch what happens.

9. At all times make sure you have food at hand.

10. If you want the whistle to be 100% reliable, never blow it and not reward, in fact when she responds to it first time, I would suggest you jackpot her. This will increase the value of the whistle sound.

Once she is responding to the whistle every time, try it in your garden when she is busy sniffing around. If she doesn't respond straight away, back up a step or two and take it back indoors for a day or two, until she becomes more reliable, then try again. Remember pay up and pay well **every time**.

Over a short period of time, your dog will see the value of the whistle sound as very important. If you want the whistle to be 100% reliable, do not be tempted to use it without rewarding with a treat your dog values for coming to you when she hears the whistle, or the value of the whistle will become less important and your dog may stop responding to it.

Dog Trainer's Notes

○ I have never taught Whistle Taining in a class environment, but there is no reason why you can't if it is your desire to.

○ I would however recommend that each owner and dog does it, one at a time in the class as it could be very confusing for the dogs, and very noisy for you and everyone else.

○ I generally give the Whistle Training exercise out as a complimentary handout, to help with the recall training that we teach in class. An additional method is always beneficial, and I take a few minutes out of a session to describe the mechanics of teaching whistle training in a session. Many of the owners in my classes taught it at home and found it very beneficial.

○ It is important to remind the owners that they must always, always reward when their dog returns after hearing the whistle, or it will invalidate the whistle and make it unimportant.

NOTES

In this Chapter

- o It's a funny old game
- o Dog Trainer's Notes
- o Teaching Retrieve
- o Location, Location
- o Keeping it fun
- o The Play Retrieve – Tug-o-war
- o Motivating your dog to play
- o The Formal Retrieve – Hold, Pick Up, Give

It's a funny old game

For many people the image of a dog retrieving a ball is the most natural thing in the world. For many dogs, the idea of retrieving a ball, something they have caught and giving it to someone else, is the most unnatural thing and goes completely against the grain of a dog's 'natural instinct'.

To chase a ball, may be instinctual for many dogs, it is after all, a moving object and it will play to many dog's prey drive, (some more so than others) the thrill of the chase, but for many once that ball ceases moving, it is dead and no longer requires their attention, or they should take it to where it's safe from others (in this case you) and tend to it.

For many dog breeds, such as gundogs, or many of the working breeds, chasing and fetching can be as natural as a duck is to water. For others, they just don't see the point or have the desire. Which category does your dog fit into?

Assess Your Dogs Retrievability

Is your dog a Bertie The Bassett Hound?

1. You throw the ball and Bertie watches it go, looks at you with an expression that says, why did you do that? Then heads off in a different direction to have a much-preferred sniff around.

Is your dog a Dixie the Dalmatian?

2. You throw the ball and Dixie chases after it, but as soon as she reaches it she heads off to do something much more exciting.

Is your dog a Titus the Terrier?

3. You throw the ball and Titus chases after it, grabs the ball in his mouth then runs away with it, hoping you'll chase him or hoping he'll find a quiet space where he can keep his prize, destroy it or even consume it.

Is your dog a Tinker the Tibetan Terrier?

4. You throw the ball and Tinker chases it, brings it straight back and gives it to you, but after a second or third throw, she looks at you with a quizzical expression that asks, 'Why do you keep throwing it away, you either want it or you don't perhaps you should go fetch it yourself now.

Is your dog a Luna the Labrador?

5. You throw the ball and Luna at the speed of light is on that ball and straight back to you. She is willing and able to play this game for as long as you can throw it, or as long, as she is able to keep running.

Identifying which description best describes your dog is for your benefit and to get you thinking. It doesn't really matter, which category your dog falls into, all dogs can be taught to retrieve. How much they want to play the game and how enthusiastically they play it, that's another matter, and often down to the owner and their enthusiasm for the game.

You might also want to consider the type of retrieve you want to teach your dog. Is it simply a chase the garden, and bring it back to you? Or throw the ball in the park and return to you with it for as long as you can throw it? Or are you hoping for a more formal retrieve where the dog is taught, to hold a dumbbell, (usually a Dog Training dumbbell).

The dog is taught to sit and wait, you throw the dumbbell and only goes to retrieve it when given the cue. She returns straight to you having retrieved the dumbbell and sits in front of you, presenting the dumbbell, still in her mouth, until you take the dumbbell and end the exercise.

Dog Trainer's Notes

o It is my recommendation that you use the Formal Retrieve method for teaching this in your class.

o The small steps to teaching this, makes for good bonding time for the owner/dog and is a great group exercise to teach.

o Once owner and dog reach a controlled level, you might want to do retrieves in twos in your class, so that each dog learns to only retrieve their dumbbell.

o Do not allow the use of a ball for teaching the retrieve in class, no matter how much the owner says their dog loves the ball:

   ▪ The ball cannot be controlled as it keeps rolling.
   ▪ The ball will not allow for the other steps to be taught correctly.
   ▪ Every dog in the class may want to chase the ball.
   ▪ The ball is harder for the owner to remove from the dog's mouth.

Teaching Retrieve

As with most exercises, the earlier you start teaching the better, however regardless of age, all dogs can learn to retrieve. It is a case of finding what makes them excited or interested.

Start simple, find a toy your dog enjoys, it's easy with a puppy, most puppies will chase anything that moves, and most puppies love to pick up and carry things in their mouths, building on this natural behaviour, is a good start for retrieve training.

Location, Location

The location I choose for beginning to teach a play retrieve, is always indoors and if possible a narrow area, something like a hallway or narrow kitchen. This minimises the distractions for your dog and prevents her from running off and gives her only two directions to work with, away from you to get what you throw and back to you with the dumbbell.

I prefer to use a long, light line on my dog, as it helps in shaping the dog's behaviour, by encouraging her to always come back to me straightaway, as some dogs will choose to stay where they collect the toy, which is not ideal as you then must go to them, to get the toy from them and this kind off defeats the object of the exercise. The long line, will allow you some control over where you want your dog to go, which should always be straight back to you.

With minimal effort you will have shaped the result you want, simply by using a long line and encouraging the dog back to you, each time she has run out and picked up her toy, in no time at all this will become a habit for your dog.

Keep it fun

If you want a happy retriever, do not introduce sits when your dog runs back to you with the toy, or insist that your dog gives up the toy too soon. Having to follow other instructions too soon after getting hold of their prize, can dampen a dog's enthusiasm. Particularly with some breeds more than others, as in the case of a breed like mine, the Tibetan Terrier. If you make the game too serious too soon, with too many rules they will simply say, 'I'd rather not play this thank you'.

So, pay close attention to what your dog is saying to you, keep the early stages of retrieve, fetch and give fun, with the emphasis on the run out and bringing it in your direction, without too much of a fuss being made over how long she holds it for, or how she gives it to you.

I like to break the retrieve down into smaller steps for teaching, and master each step individually, before putting them together. This may seem like a very long process, but it is not, as many of these steps should be part of your everyday interaction with your dog, this is the fastest way of teaching a sound, fast and accurate retrieve, that your dog just loves to share with you.

It is also worth mentioning that if you are not someone who likes repetitive games, then perhaps teaching retrieve is not the best exercise for you to teach your dog, because you can be certain that once learnt, your dog will ask you to engage in this game, when they are bored, when they think you need cheering up, when you have work to do, and when you least have time. It can be hard to say no to your dog, when they have learnt to love this time with you and they believe you love it too.

The Play Retrieve

Tug-o-war

If you want your dog to enjoy play retrieving with you then you need to get to work on spending quality time playing with her. There is no better way than playing a game of Tug-o-war to get your dog enthusiastic about a toy.

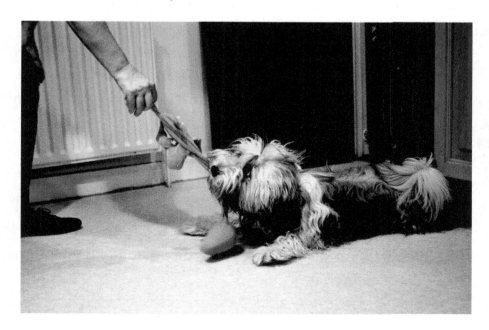

This game is frowned upon by many as a game of strength and dominance, however I prefer to see this game as an opportunity. An opportunity for you and your dog to bond and to get to know one another, an opportunity for your dog to learn the rules of the game. Like any good game, knowing the rules is essential for the correct outcome to be achieved.

There is much more to a game of Tug-o-war than you might think and one of the reasons I like to teach Tug-o-war is, if your dog learns to love the game of Tug-o-war, there is a good chance that she will run out and fetch that toy naturally, in the hope that you will Tug again with her.

In my book 'Pre-Vaccination Puppy Training', when I wrote about Tug-o-war, I said, 'When you play Tug-o-war, do not let your puppy wander off with the toy', I should have added to this, 'Depending on the puppy (and this is where it's helpful to know your puppy's character, and their likes and dislikes) some dogs are reluctant players, or sensitive and a little reluctant. If the dog with this character never gets to win, they may decide they don't want to play the game, as no one likes to constantly be defeated, what fun is there in that.

Mr Tibs—Training Tip

It is worth mentioning at this stage, to have a dog who is enthusiastic about retrieve, you need to play the game regularly if not daily, for them to get the point of it and to learn it is fun.

If you are not prepared to commit the time and dedication it requires from you as your dog's play-mate, they will not see the point in it, and they will look at you with a very quizzical expression when you suddenly pick up a toy and throw it and demand that they fetch it.

It will do no harm to let this type of dog take the toy from your hand, to show off her trophy. Make a huge fuss telling her she's wonderful, you'll be surprised how a little success breeds enthusiasm for your dog to work a bit harder to win the game.

What toy makes a good tug toy?

Many dogs will tug on just about anything you try to pull from them, however there are also dogs who are very specific about what they will not pull on, or even pick up. My own dogs don't like rubber toys, they are put off by the smell, so a rubber ring or a rubber tug toys would be the furthest down the list of things to pull for my dogs.

This really will be trial and error. Most dogs will tug on a soft toy, but most soft toys are not going to stand up to the rigours of canine teeth for very long.

There are some excellent toys on the market though and the following is by no means comprehensive, these toys are offered as a guage for you to work from.

A tug toy needs to be long enough so that you can avoid contact with those strong teeth, in case your dog misjudges grabbing hold of the toy for your hand. This is an obvious hazard of playing this game, as they can get very excited, until they have learnt your rules of the game.

Setting up the game of Tug-o-War

1. The toy that you have chosen as your tug toy, should be kept for just that.

2. Keep the toy in your possession so that your dog can't access it (put the toy in a cupboard, drawer or box) and your dog only gets to play with the toy, when you play with it together.

3. This makes the toy much more exciting and the dog's desire to get it will be much greater, a) It belongs to you. b) It is your special time together and c) They always want what they can't have.

4. If you leave the toy lying around, the toy will lose its value and interest for your dog.

5. Play short sessions of tug and end the game when the dog is still interested in play, don't keep playing until the dog is fed up, as that is the last thing she will remember. It is important to leave her wanting more.

6. Decide which end of the toy is yours and which end is hers, do not allow her to take your end of the toy.

Cue words for Tug-o-war

Get it – Means for your dog to grab hold of the toy in her mouth.

Pull or Tuggies – Means to pull on the toy. Choose which cue you want to use as your cue word and stick with it.

Off, Give, or Out – means to let go straight away. Choose which cue you want to use as yours and stick with it. *Notice I did not use 'Leave it, or Drop it'. This is because these two words mean a completely different thing, as taught in this book. It is important to keep a clear distinction between these two words.*

Leave it – Means, Do Not under any circumstances touch it, this is a very serious instruction that could save your dog's life one day, as whatever they are contemplating touching could be poison or cause a serious problem for your dog, if they get hold of it.

Drop it – Means to spit it out straight away and you don't want them to give it to you.

These two cues **Leave it** or **Drop it**, should be able to be given from a distance as needing to be by your dog, for them to respond, could be too late to save their lives.

Why are so many different words necessary? You are probably asking yourself this question, especially if you are a dog trainer. My answer is, I believe it is essential to teach different words if you want your dog to understand without question, and without making a mistake, that for some words there is absolutely no room for questioning. Understanding these words, could make the difference between your dog surviving and your dog dying one day. Teaching the 'Leave it' or 'Drop it', is dealt with in the chapter 'Food Refusal'.

For now, we are concentrating on the fun element of letting go of a toy. The training is very different.

Playing the game

Rule 1 - Show your dog the tug toy, make it exciting when you introduce the toy. When she puts her mouth on it, say, **'Get It'**. You are teaching her that by putting her mouth on the toy, the cue word is, **'Get It'**. Every time she takes the toy in her mouth, you are going to say, **'Get It.'** When she takes

the toy in her mouth, you are going to tell her she is a 'Good dog'. It won't take long for her to understand what this means. Repetition is key, as it is for all training.

Rule 2 - Once your dog has the toy in her mouth, she will most likely start to tug on it, as she is tugging introduce the cue word, pull/pullies or tuggies, whichever you prefer. Keep telling her how good she is, as she is pulling.

Rules 1 and 2 are the easy bits for most dogs.

Rule 3 – Stick to your own end or the toy, can sometimes be challenging.

Rule 3 – Stick to your own end. One end of the tug to is your dog's to hold and the other end, usually the handle, is yours. Under no circumstances do you let your dog determine which end she gets to hold. If when she's tugging you notice your dog is gradually working her way up the toy to take hold of your end, stop the game.

How to stop the game

Keep hold of the toy and move your hands down the toy until you reach where the dog is holding it, keep your hands still, ideally if you can put your hands close to her muzzle and hold on there without pulling, she should at some point let go, as soon as she lets go,

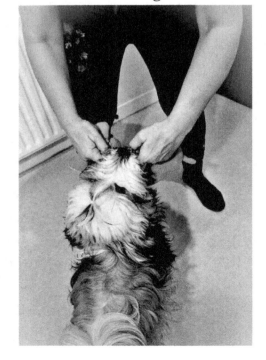

say **'Give'**, make a huge fuss of her, reposition the toy and start play again.

Rule 4 – 'Give' can be more challenging for many dog owners to achieve. Once you have taught this to your dog, this game takes on a whole new meaning and you can have so much fun with it. Simply tugging on a toy, is not as much fun for us feeble owners as it is for the dog, particularly if you have a Hercules of a dog to play with, although it is surprising how even a small dog can muster an enormous amount of strength when they want to keep that toy. Teaching them to let go on cue is so much more enjoyable for you both.

Playing by the rules will tire your dog so much more than simply pulling, as they will have to use their brain to follow the rules. They will become both mentally and physically tired after playing a 10 minute tug game with you.

As soon as she has given it to you, tell her to **'Get it'** and let the game commence. *The best reward you can give a dog, is whatever it was doing before you interrupted them. I.e. Your dog is tugging, and you ask her to give, she leaves the toy immediately, tell her she's good and resume play instantly. In her mind, it is worth giving up the toy, as she gets to play straight away again.*

Repetition is key here and I'm sure your dog would thank you if she could, for a daily game of Tug-o-war.

Once your dog is keen to play Tug-o-war, quite often throwing it on the floor is enough for your dog to pick it up and present it straight back to your hand, after all, she can't play tuggies on her own and playing with someone is much more exciting than playing on her own. This will be the beginnings of your Play Retrieve. Gradually increase the distance you throw the toy to see how game your dog is to fetch it and bring it back to you.

Mr Tibs — Training Tip

For some dogs, games are only as exciting as the person they are playing with.

If you are not enthusiastic about the game, you can be sure your dog won't be either.

Motivating your dog to play

So, your dog has no interest in playing with toys and retrieving is proving difficult?

o   Know your dog – How interested is your dog in the game?

o   Choose a toy that interests your dog, what you might find exciting, may not be your dog's choice.

o   For dogs who are not motivated by toys, sometimes you need to get a little creative. Sometimes an old cloth with a knot in it is more exciting than any toy, like and old tea towel, or an old sock with a knot in it.

- Tease your dog with your chosen toy, by wiggling it on the floor and even touching the dog with it.

- Sometimes it can take a lot of effort on the owner's part to stimulate the non-play dog. You might feel like you are getting nowhere, but just keep trying and trust me, at some point your dog will want to join you in the fun.

- Playing with the toy with another person, throwing it to one another can sometimes create an interest.

- Make sure if your dog shows any interest in the toy at all they can get it, if you keep it to yourself they will lose interest.

- Go wild with excitement if they pick the toy up.

- Sometimes attaching string to a toy and running it round the floor, can work with the dog's natural prey drive and stimulate them to chase it.

- Rubbing a tasty treat on the toy can stimulate their senses to show more interest in the toy.

Dog Trainer's Notes

The formal retrieve is the perfect exercise to be encouraged in a class.

Each dog will require their own dumbbell a) To fit their muzzle, and b) Many dogs won't want to put a dumbbell in their mouth that smells of another dog.

You should explain to the class that the formal retrieve can take months to teach, they must be patient and not try to rush.

It is a great bonding exercise for owner and dog and nothing is more impressive than a dog who knows all the steps to display a perfectly controlled retrieve.

The Formal / Controlled Retrieve

The Formal/Control Retrieve (or Dead Retrieve, as it's sometimes known, basically means it's static, you don't throw **the dumbbell** to teach it), is what you would see in an obedience competition if you've ever watched one.

The dumbbell used to teach the 'Formal Retrieve' should be something that the dog has never played with. In the formal retrieve, we don't want the dog to learn to chew on the dumbbell like they would with a toy. They are taught to run out, pick it up and hold it steady in their mouth until you take it from them.

Mr Tibs — Training Tip

You can clicker train this if you prefer. Simply substitute the 'Yes', for the clicker.

For this reason, it is good to choose something that the dog would not associate with tearing or chewing on. My item of choice is a Dog Training dumbbell, you can choose something that is different if you think it is appropriate, however dumbbells are readily available on the internet, if you choose to use one. The dumbbell you choose, will never be used as a play toy and never left lying around where the dog may get it and chew on it. This helps in communicating to your dog that this is different, and it has a specific purpose.

There is no problem with teaching the Formal Retrieve and the Play Retrieve, simultaneously.

They are both taught differently, it's like teaching a completely different exercise, the one exercise will not confuse the other.

5 Steps to a Formal Retrieve

Step 1. Hold

Step 2. Pick up and Present

Step 3. Give

Step 4. Fetch/Retrieving the object

**Step 5.
Putting all The Steps Together**

The Hold

The 'Hold' is the key to this whole exercise. We are going to teach the hold by using our Target training info, just as we did for the Touch Stick. What does hold mean? Hold means taking the dumbbell in their mouth, without chewing  it or tossing it around, and 'hold it still', until asked to 'give it up'.

The old traditional method for teaching this, was to open the dogs mouth and place the dumbbell into the dog's mouth and prevent the dog from spitting it out, a second at a time until the dog accepted it, gradually increasing the time they held it for.

There is no doubt that this method worked, but dogs hate it. They have no choice over it, and for many dogs it was a real battle of wills between dog and owner until the dog gave in. I don't remember ever seeing a dog learn by this method who was happy at the time. So, I never found this an acceptable or an enjoyable means of teaching a dog retrieve or any other exercise for that matter, but at the time it was all I had to go with, I was new to training and under instruction from other dog trainers.

When I started teaching my own classes, I avoided teaching it for many years as my memories of it just weren't good, even though my dogs were brilliant at completing the formal retrieve. I did not want other pet dogs to have to learn something through force, this was not a life or death exercise, this was supposed to be fun.

Fortunately, not many pet owners were interested in this and therefore having no requests for it, meant I side stepped it very nicely. Until one year I decided it was time to find a new method for teaching it, and target training was the obvious choice.

My TT's really did not like being taught the hold the traditional way, which is not surprising as I'm certain no one would like to have something put in their mouth and made to hold it against their will. Until I taught my TT's they had a choice, using targeting, things started to change. Once they made the choice to take the article for themselves, we never looked back.

Since using the targeting method for teaching it, all have taken to it enthusiastically, albeit a little slower in reaching the final result, but much happier in their working attitude towards it, and much more pleasant training sessions for us both.

Mr Tibs — Training Tip

Remember, Target training is all about rewarding the smallest of steps, to encourage the dog in any effort in the right direction. Keep the target simple.

I always teach retrieve by keeping the retrieve item (in this case my dumbbell) in my hand. Never by throwing it at this stage. Throwing it comes only when the dog has learnt all the elements of the retrieve and you can put it all together. This prevents the dog from making mistakes with it, i.e. batting it about with their feet, tossing it, or chewing it etc. All problems you would have to solve, once you have let them start. Remember prevention is better than cure.

Teaching the Hold

Begin sitting on a chair or your couch and have your dog sit in front of you. Try to keep them sitting as it makes things easier to monitor, control and keeps your dog calm. Your dog will always start the retrieve in a sit by your side, but for now we just need her to stay sitting in front of you until  things get going and she understands some of what you are asking.

Step 1. Arm yourself with a pouch full of treats, hold the dumbbell in your hand and bring it down to the dog's nose level.

Step 2. As soon as the dog sniffs the dumbbell, say 'Yes' to mark the behaviour and reward. Remember the 'Yes', should come before the food reward.

Step 3. Repeat steps 1 and 2 until your dog is repeatedly touching the dumbbell with her nose, or lips. *(There is no need for a cue word at this time)*.

Step 4. Move the goal post slightly, this time hold the dumbbell in front of your dog and wait for her to touch it, twice before moving the dumbbell away. You are basically looking for more effort from your dog. In holding the dumbbell in place for a few moments, this allows space for  your dog to experiment with what it is you want. As soon as she touches twice, say, 'Yes' to mark the behaviour and then food reward.

Step 5. If at any point your dog opens her mouth and touches the dumbbell with her teeth, however little, grab this behaviour with the 'Yes' marker and reward her well.

Step 6. Once your dog starts to put her mouth on it, stop rewarding the touching with the nose, and only reward mouth contact with it. *Do not let her take the dumbbell and run off with it, as this will undo all your hard work. Keep hold of the dumbbell at all times, to encourage her to stay calm and controlled.*

Step 7. It's now time to move your dog to your side. Lead your dog to your left-hand side and ask them to Sit. Repeat from Step 1, with your dog in a sit on your left-hand side, until you have achieved steps 1 to 5 at your side. Your dog will always work from this position from now on.

Mr Tibs — Training Tip

At no point do you allow your dog to run off with the dumbbell, it must stay firmly in your hand.

Step 8. You will gradually increase the length of time you require your dog to hold the dumbbell for. Hold the dumbbell by one end, and place at least 2 of your fingers under the centre dowel, supporting the dumbbell by resting your dog's chin on your fingers, when she has the dumbbell in her mouth. Only expect a couple of seconds

to begin with, then mark the behaviour with 'Yes' and follow through with a treat reward.

The hardest bit of this exercise is complete, in my opinion. To get your dog to open her mouth and want to take the dumbbell, is the biggest challenge, the rest of the exercise will follow with time and patience.

Cueing the hold

Now that your dog can open her mouth and take the dumbbell for a second, it's time to introduce the cue word. Every time she opens her mouth to take it, say **'Hold'** and then say **'Give'**, as you take it back. Repeat as often as you can, until you think she is starting to understand what you want her to do.

To test her understanding, bring the dumbbell down to her mouth level, and without bringing it to her, say **'Hold'** watch for any movement towards the dumbbell to attempt to hold it, reward any effort, with an exciting **'Yes'** and lots of praise, reward well.

Once your dog is reaching forward to the 'Hold dumbbell', it is now time to lower your hand slowly towards the floor. Inch by inch lower the dumbbell to the floor, keeping your hand always on the dumbbell to prevent your dog from making mistakes.

Teaching Give

Teaching **'Give'**, does not usually prove a problem, as you will have taught this inadvertently while teaching the **'Hold'**. However, occasionally as trainers we come across a dog who simply loves to take control of the dumbbell and refuses to give it back. When this happens, it's time to do a swapsy, you are going to swap what your dog has for either, another dumbbell (exactly the same), or a high value treat. This may need a little trial and error on your part, to find out which your dog prefers.

Do not wrestle your dog for it, as this may be what she would like you to do, particularly if you have taught her tug-o-war.

Every time you take the Dumbbell from your dog's mouth, say the cue word, 'Give'. It won't take long for your dog to make the connection that giving the object to you is called, 'Give'.

Pick Up and Present

Step 1. With your dog in a Sit on your left side, ask your dog to wait, while you place your holding dumbbell on the floor 1 step in front of you. Take a step forward with your right foot and place the dumbbell to the left of your right foot on an angle, *(as in picture, this is to make the pick up easier for your dog as she comes around your leg)*.

Step 2. Take your left foot forward toward the dumbbell, at the same time cueing your dog to 'Hold', take your hand down towards the dumbbell, to encourage your dog, until she is clear what it is you are wanting her to do.

Step 3. Your dog will hopefully move towards the dumbbell and pick it up, as she lifts it, encourage her by guiding her to turn towards you. Your Left foot is there to encourage your dog to go around it, before picking up the dumbbell, this is to teach your dog to always go behind the dumbbell to pick up, this stops the dog from

Mr Tibs—Training Tip

It is important to not let your dog drop the dumbbell, so make sure your hands are always by it to catch it and always say, 'Give' when you take it and 'Hold' when it is in your dog's mouth.

diving on to it, when she eventually runs out to retrieve it and knocking it across the floor. The technical term for this, is 'A Clean Pick Up. It also helps to set the dog up for coming in a straight line back to you as she is already facing you when she picks up.

Taught accurately this gives us what is termed as a 'clean pickup'.

Repeat steps 1 to 3, until you are confident your dog knows what you want from her. Some dogs may struggle with this transition at first, and they may require you to put your hand under the dumbbell, before they will pick it up, this is because they have been conditioned to take the dumbbell from your hands.

Fetch/Retrieve

You are on the home stretch with this now, so don't give up, it is such a beautiful thing when it all comes together. You will be so proud.

Although this is a fetch or a retrieve, I prefer to keep the cue, 'Hold' as the trigger for your dog to go out and get it, this keeps in her mind that she is not to play with it, but to handle the dumbbell as she has been taught. The cue Fetch should be saved for the play retrieve that we taught earlier.

Step 1. Dog on your left side ask your dog to wait, go two paces in front of you and place the dumbbell in a straight position on the floor, return to your dog and stand beside her.

Step 2. Give your dog the cue to 'Hold', in a happy tone, at the same time step forward with your left leg to encourage your dog to go forward.

Step 3. As soon as she has the dumbbell in her mouth, step back and ask her to come to you.

Step 4. When your dog reaches you, ask her to Sit and Hold. If she sits and keeps hold of the dumbbell, take it straight away and make a huge fuss, lots of praise.

Step 5. Repeat steps 1 to 4 at each training session, when your dog is happily going two paces and picking up, increase to 3 then 4 etc.

Only when your dog is travelling 'consistently' to the placed dumbbell, going behind it, picking it up, bringing it straight to you can you begin to consider throwing it for her. However, if when you begin throwing it she gets over excited and starts kicking it about, not going behind it to pick up, or running around with it, then you must calm it down and go back to placing the dumbbell. In most training sessions, I would only throw the dumbbell once, the rest of the time I would place it, to prevent mistakes from happening.

Congratulations, you now have a completed 'Formal Retrieve', you should be extremely proud of yourself and your dog.

Remember: For some dogs, games are only as exciting as the person they are playing with. If you are not enthusiastic about the game, you can be sure your dog won't be either.

Mr Tibs — Training Tip

Remember to not throw the dumbbell, it is far too soon. Place the dumbbell only! Until your dog is perfect at going out picking up.

13 Target Training with the Touch Stick

In this Chapter

- o What is Target Training
- o Teaching Touch with the Nose
- o Teaching Touch with the Paw
- o Dog Trainer's Notes

What is Target Training?

Target training is a very useful and fun exercise. It is excellent to teach in class situations, as well as for the individual at home. It is taught

Ace—Top Trick
No Previous Training required

Target Training is one of the best exercises you can teach a dog. It opens up the world of learning for the dog, once it understands it.

using a target stick, you can buy purpose made fold out target sticks, but I much prefer my own homemade target stick.

A Piece of dowel about the length of your arm. On each end of the

dowel, I put some tape, a different colour for each end. One end will be for your dog's nose and the other for her paws. Your dog will learn to identify each end and whether they should touch or tap it.

With their nose the cue will be 'Touch' and their paw will be 'Tap'. The colours I use are red and yellow, I use red for nose and yellow for paw, but you can choose whatever works for you. The touch stick is a great exercise for developing your dog's brain and for creating a mentally tired and contented dog.

Teaching Touch/Targeting with the Nose.

Stage 1

The excess of the target stick, should be tucked under your arm, with the red tape end held in your hand.

Step 1. Bring your hand with the tape end in it down to a level your dog can reach easily.

Step 2. If she shows any interest in looking at or approaching your hand, say 'Yes' — Yes marks the behaviour, telling your dog that this is what you want her to do. Take your hand away so that she can no longer reach it, this prevents her from making mistakes. Reward with a treat straight away, this is your secondary reinforcer, the 'Yes' word being your primary reinforcer.

Step 3. Repeat these steps rapidly several times, until your dog is consistently touching your hand and looking at you for her reward.

Step 4. You will know she is starting to understand what it is you want, when she touches your hand and looks straight at your face.

Step 5. Keep the end of the stick concealed in your hand, until you reach this last stage. This will prevent her from mouthing at the stick, preventing unwanted problems or behaviours from occurring.

Prevention is always better than cure. As your dog becomes clear what it is you want, they tend to get excited and this is when the mouthing can start.

Summary for Stage 1

Have treats and target stick ready.

Say nothing to your dog.

Hold one end of the stick in the palm of your hand, I hold the red end, as this will be her nose target.

Remember one end/one colour of the stick is for nose touching and the other end/colour for paw tapping.

Bring your hand with stick down to a level that is easy to reach for your dog.

As your dog reaches to your hand to sniff, mark the behaviour by saying 'Yes' in a happy tone.

Remove your stick hand instantly you have said 'Yes', so that she can no longer reach it and reward.

Mr Tibs — Training Tip

Minimising mistakes

1. How much stick you show the dog at the beginning, prevents the dog from wanting to mouth it.

2. Remove the stick each time the dog has achieved the target, while you reward. This prevents the dog becoming too familiar too quickly and making mistakes.

Repeat 10 times or until your dog becomes consistent in reaching for your hand, every time.

Once she is reliably touching your hand, open your hand so that she can see what is in it, but keep the stick in your palm.

Repeat the exercises exactly as before until she is reliably touching the end of the stick and looking at you for confirmation.

Mr Tibs—Training Tip

o Remember to move the stick around encouraging your dog to travel to reach it.

o As soon as she connects with it, say 'Yes', move the stick away so that she can no longer touch it until you have rewarded her.

Problem Busting for the Touch Stick

Question: Your dog ignores your hand and the stick, what should you do?

Take a tasty treat, something with a strong smell and rub it over the tape end of the stick. Be ready with your marker word, 'Yes' and a treat. Her attention is sure to be drawn to it, straight away. Strong smelly treats might include liver or sausage.

Hiding the stick hand behind your back will increase your dog's curiosity about it, making her far more likely to sniff it when presented with it.

Extending the target stick – Stage 2

Step 1. Move the tape end that has been concealed in your palm, just outside of your hand. At this stage it is important that the dog is rewarded 'only' for touching the tape on the stick.

Step 2. Your timing is crucial, your 'Yes' word that marks the behaviour must be given as soon as she touches the tape. Do not say yes if she touches anywhere other than the tape on the stick.

Step 3. Once she is consistently touching the tape, you can extend the stick further to her.

Step 4. More of the stick is extended now. It is important more than ever to maintain control over where the dog touches on the stick, preventing her from making mistakes, so that she is prevented from becoming random where she touches.

The Final Result

To have your dog follow the stick to any position, touching only the tape end and the stick should be extended to a full arms-length, with your dog happy to follow it, wherever you move it to.

Teaching Targeting with the Paw

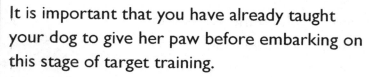

The other end of your stick should have a different colour tape on it, this will be your dog's signal that this tape is for paw only as she learns.

Ace—Top Trick

It is important that you have already taught your dog to give her paw before embarking on this stage of target training.

You will need: A dog, Food, a Target stick

As in step by step teaching the nose target, you are going to hold the stick in a similar manner.

Step 1. Start by holding the stick tucked under your arm, with the second colour tape end held in your hand.

Step 2. Bring your hand with the tape end in it, down to a level your dog can reach easily with her paw.

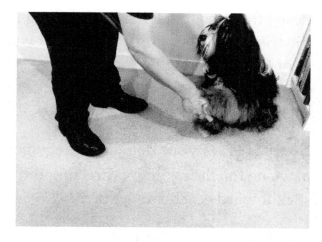

Step 3. Because you have already taught paw, you can save time, by giving your dog the paw cue. If she shows any interest in touching your hand, say 'Yes'. Don't forget, 'Yes' marks the correct behaviour, telling your dog that this is what you want her to do. Take your hand and stick away, so that she can no longer reach it, this prevents her from making mistakes.

Step 4. Reward with a treat straight away, this is your secondary reinforcer, the 'Yes' word being your primary reinforcer.

Step 5. Repeat these steps rapidly several times, until your dog is consistently touching your hand and looking at you for her reward.

Step 6. You will know she is starting to understand what it is you want, when she touches your hand and looks straight at your face.

Step 7. One she is pawing your hand as soon as you present it, extend the stick further, revealing the tape, point the stick further towards your dog's paw, giving her a chance to get it right and blocking attempts to touch it with her nose.

Resist the urge to tell her she's wrong if she tries to use her nose, you do not want to put her off using her nose. Simply don't reward on these occasions, take the stick out of reach and try again.

Step 8. Have your dog alternate which paw she touches with by directing the stick towards each paw in turn.

Step 9. As she taps the stick with her paw, cue your dog **Tap Left, Tap Right**.

Mr Tibs—Training Tip

Now your dog has mastered Touching with her nose and Tapping with her paws, practice alternating the ends of the stick and be amazed that your dog has learnt the cues for each tape colour.

Dog Trainers Notes

o This is a wonderful exercise to teach in a class situation.

o Ideally have target sticks to give to your class, either to use in class or to purchase if they don't want to make their own.

o The class can work at this at the same time, while you wander around to observe their progress.

o There should be no commands/cues given to the dog. The dog should be taught to offer the behaviour, not wait to be instructed.

NOTES

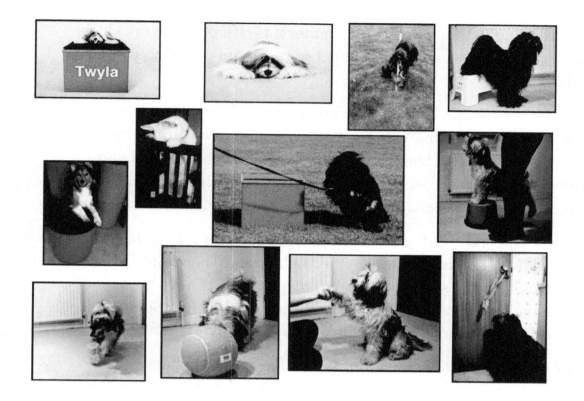

In this Chapter

- o For the Dog Trainer
- o Box Work
- o Go Round
- o Behind
- o Left Paw Right Paw – on the box
- o Off the box
- o Both paws on the box (while sitting)
- o Step up on the box (Front paws only)
- o Head down
- o Hide your eyes using the box
- o Get on the box and sit

It doesn't matter what you teach your dog, if, they are physically capable of doing it, they don't care whether it is a sit or a hop on 3 legs, they love to please you and you will get so much out of seeing your dog achieve.

The variety of exercises available for you and your dog to learn, are endless. Whatever you enjoy doing, you can guarantee your dog will too. The more you teach her, the more likely she is to be fulfilled and contented and the more likely she is to want to be with you as her friend, companion, play-mate and leader.

When I first opened the doors of Ace K9 in 2005, a shop front training, behaviour and grooming centre, on the High Street. The variety of classes I taught in my school was quite unique and I believe the first of its kind in the UK offering this type of training on the High Street. All, the exercises written here, are exercises I taught in my Training School.

They are exercises I guarantee your dog will love learning and want to share in the experience with you. This is by no means comprehensive, but your dog will love learning something new. These exercises are simple but fun for your dog to learn with you.

Whether you are a Dog Trainer or a Pet Owner, I hope you find some inspiration from them and find something different for your class or your own dog, that you might not have thought of before.

- If you are a dog trainer, I would most definitely encourage you to teach these exercises to your classes (if you don't already), the dogs will love them and so too will the owner.

- Dog owners just love watching their dog achieve, don't we? You will get so much pleasure from teaching these exercises and people certainly won't want to leave your training school in a hurry.

- They will be having so much fun and they will be so impressed with the repertoire the dog has learnt. You will also find a lot of owners rise to the challenge of working harder with their dog, as they won't want people out doing them, watching how well the other dog learns. A little competition is a good thing.

Keep it fun, fresh and exciting for both dog and owner

- Take a chance and try something new. Thinking outside the box can make a difference to more owners and to more dogs.

- It is important to make training fun, right? After all, there are only so many sit, downs and stays that a clever animal like the dog will want to do, before they lose interest in wanting to practice.

- I also find that owners lose interest if training is not exciting and varied. The more variety you teach them, the more they will stay interested in you and your school. Even with the Kennel Club Good Citizen Scheme incorporated into your classes, you can still manage to add in these extra fun games. Going that extra step with your classes makes all the difference between a good Training School, and an **excellent** Training School

Box work

What is box work?

The box is a tool that allows you to engage your dog in many ways, to learn many different behaviours using one tool. Box work is a whole lot of simple fun and dogs love it.

The box can be a plastic toy box turned upside down or a sturdy foot-stool. The box I use is made from wood with rubber glued to the top to stop the dog's feet from slipping, you can equally use carpet for the top. I had a very kind client offer to make me some aluminium drums, these were super for training on. With a little creativity, you can create something that you can work with at home.

There are so many exercises you can teach using a box. The first simple exercise we are going to teach your dog, is to 'Go Round'. This is where you send the dog away from you to go run around the box and back to you (see Picture 1).

Go Round

Why teach Go Round?
Cue Word - 'Go Round'

The first exercise I teach using the box has always been to Go Round it.

Picture 1

As well as for the fun of it, there are some benefits to teaching this exercise, imagine you are out walking and your dog goes the opposite direction to you, around a lamp post or a tree, while on the lead. You

Ace — Top Trick

No previous training required

Selecting the right box is important. Not too high, not too low, just right!

can use your cue, 'Go Round' and your dog will know, how to untangle themselves. I know what you're thinking, 'but I could just untangle the lead for them', which is fine if you have only one dog, but imagine like me you have 5 or 6 dogs with you, it doesn't take long before you can get in a real muddle with leads, if one dog takes a wrong turn and how much more exciting is it, when your dog knows exactly what you are saying and how to execute the cue, making things easier for you both. It is very helpful and most impressive watching your dog problem solve.

A little story for you as an example of how training such an exercise can be such a useful and a rewarding experience for you and your dog.

My first Tibetan Terrier Mr Tibs, started to go blind at 7 years old, he developed a condition called Primary Lens Luxation (PLL). PLL was accompanied by another condition called Glaucoma. Unfortunately for him, this too was primary, it was fairly unusual for dogs as it is more commonly seen in horses. Unfortunately, by the time Mr Tibs was 9 years old he had both his eyes removed. I was devastated.

He was such a special dog and taught me so much about how different breeds of dogs can be. Mr Tibs remained rather unique among dogs as we opted to have artificial eye implants put in, rather than take the eyes

179

out and close the sockets up. We never regretted it for one moment.

Mr Tibs was my working partner and he was a highly skilled trickster, everything from Riding a skate board to running on 3 legs on cue.

'Go Round', 'Walk Back' and 'Step Up', became three of the most useful commands in his days with no sight. He would regularly find himself stuck under a table or behind a door and with the guidance of one of these cue's he knew, I could help him out of most situations, without having to get hold of him and lead him out. I was so glad that he knew so many cues and was such a happy boy.

Tibs lived until he was 16 with his blindness, he was diabetic and had 3 strokes, recovering from each one until we had to make that dreadful decision on the last stroke. For most of his time he was very happy, with a real sense of humour and loved by all who met and knew him. His bond and trust in me was immense, he even made his final Television appearance performing with no eye sight. Riding a skateboard and being exactly where he needed to be on cue, because of the training and respect he had. Another story for another book!

Mr Tibs — Training Tip

It is important that the box is sturdy enough that it will not topple or collapse when your dog places their feet on it.

It is also important that you place the box on a non-slip surface so that it does not slide when your dog steps onto it.

Treats — Pay up and pay well.

Keep it fast and fun and keep it simple.

Teaching Go Round

Step 1. Have your dog by your left side, with a treat in your hand, encourage your dog by luring with the treat to follow it around the box and back to you.

Step 2. Repeat until your dog starts to get the idea of what you want. The more fun and energy you put into this, the more your dog will enjoy it and the faster she will do it.

Step 3. As your dog is going around the box, give the cue, 'Go Round'. She will quickly begin to make the connection between the movement and the cue.

Step 4. The aim is to be able to send your dog to any object and to go around it and back to you on cue.

Behind

Cue word: 'Behind'

I just love when my dog understands what it is to go behind an object and just sit or stand there. There is something very simple but satisfying in having my dog understand this Try it and enjoy the moment when your dog understands two words with the same object. 'Go Round' means to travel all the way round the box and back to you. 'Behind', means to go to the back of the box and sit behind it.

Mr Tibs—Training Tip

Teach **Behind** and **Go Round** separately to avoid confusing your dog. **Go Round** should be taught <u>before</u> **Behind**.

Teaching 'Behind'

Step 1. Have your dog by your left side, with a treat in your hand.

Step 2. Encourage your dog by luring with the treat to follow it around to the back of the box. Stop with the treat held behind the box and ask your dog to sit.

Step 3. Make a huge fuss of her, so that she knows she has got it right. Reward her with a tasty treat.

Step 4. Call her back to you away from the box.

Step 5. Repeat steps 1 to 3 until the dog starts to respond to the cue.

- Go Round and Behind, are simple fun exercises to teach, but very satisfying.
- It may be a good idea to purchase some simple stepping stools or if you know a handy man/woman, have some boxes made that your class can have at hand to work with.
- Some inexpensive stepping stools, like the type used for children to step up onto are really good and will be adequate for most of these exercises. Although they will be a bit low for the dog to learn to hide it's eyes and to get up onto it. You might want to hold this in mind when looking at suitable items, different size dogs will call for different size boxes.
- Ask owners to consider bringing their own. If they get creative, they can carry all their props in it.

Head Down on the box.

Cue Word – Head or Head Down

If you have already taught the head down exercise on the floor, this will be very easy for your dog and she should learn it in super quick time.

If she already knows the 'Head Down' cue, have her sit behind the box and cue her to put her head down and see what she does. You may get lucky and she'll do it straight away, if this happens, go wild with excitement telling her how amazing she is and don't forget to pay up generously with the reward.

There is the possibility that when she hears the cue she will lie down behind the box confused that the box has anything to do with the cue. This is because she learnt to do Head Down in a down on the floor. If this happens, a little bit of guidance will soon have her executing the cue with no problem.

The following steps will assist you in communicating Head Down on the box, should you need it.

Teaching Head Down on a box

Step 1. Have your dog sit behind the box (as in the previous exercise)

Step 2. Using a treat held on the top of the box, wait for your dog to reach for the treat with her chin touching the box, then reward.

Step 3. When she is consistently touching the box with her chin to receive the reward, give the cue 'Head Down', as she does it.

Step 4. If she already knew head down, she has probably made the connection already, that this is the same as what you taught her previously on the floor. If Head Down is new to her, persevere with the repetitions of touching her chin to the box, while giving the cue at the same time and she will suddenly make the connection.

Step 5. Keep the treat further away from the box, i.e. don't rest it on the box, point to the box and say Head Down and see what she does. If she doesn't respond, or looks confused, back up a step or two and give her a bit more time to practice, it won't take long for her to work things out.

Teaching Paws Up on the Box

So, you have already taught your dog to give its Paw. Teaching her to transfer giving her paw to the box, should be easy. If, however you haven't taught it, you really need to go back and teach it, to make things easier for your dog.

Left Paw, Right Paw

Cue word – Left and Right

In the Paw exercise, you taught the dog to give its paw to your hand, you are now going to teach your dog to place each paw alternatively on the box and keep it there until she hears the release command.

Step 1. Place your hand flat on top of the box, palm up and ask your dog for her paw, if she attempts to give you a paw, go wild with excitement and pay her well.

Step 2. If she doesn't offer you a paw and is hesitant because of the box, reach your hand further over the box towards her, keeping the box between you and her, hold your hand towards her paw, to make it more normal to her.

Step 3. Gradually pull your hand back and up on to the top of the box, she will probably have forgotten about the box now, while focusing on the reward.

Step 4. Gradually distance yourself from the box, beginning by standing up and asking for her paw, then gradually move backwards, until you can signal with your left and right hands alternatively to get your dog to place her paw(s) when cued.

Mr Tibs — Training Tip

It is essential that you use the 'Off' cue to teach her to remove her paws from the box when you tell her, as it can make it difficult for you to progress to other positions, without accomplishing this cue.

Both Paws on a box in a Sit

Cue word – Both Paws

We are going to teach your dog to put both paws on the box at once and to get off the box when told.

Step 1. Have your dog sit behind the box, it's important that she sits as close to the box as possible, so that she can reach with her front paws.

Step 2. Take the treat to her mouth, raising your hand slightly above her head, so that she must stretch to reach it.

Step 3. Reaching up at some point

she will lift her two paws off the floor to try and reach, as soon as those paws move from the floor, mark the behaviour with 'Yes' and reward.

Step 4. Keep practising and it won't take long before she uses the box to support her paws while she tries to reach the treat.

Step 5. Once she connects, give the cue, 'both paws', mark the behaviour with 'Yes' and reward. Keep practising until she understands when you signal and cue 'Both Paws', she does it automatically.

Step 6. Once you know she understands what you are asking, start increasing the distance you stand from the box after each few attempts at sending her, if she is getting it right.

Step Up

Cue Word – Step Up

This is pretty similar to the previous exercise, except the dog will stand with their paws up, rather than sitting. As seen in the photo with Rayna demonstrating it.

Step 1. Have your dog go behind the box, don't encourage her to sit, it is easier to teach 'Step Up' if she is standing.

Step 2. Hold a treat over the middle of the box, high enough that she can't reach it without stepping up with her front paws. You may find she moves around the box in order to try working out how to reach it. Do not worry about that at this stage, once she makes the connection that she just needs to step up to be rewarded with the treat, she will then stay behind the box.

Step 3. Encourage her to get off the box, by simply throwing a treat behind the box. She will step down to get the treat, as soon as she gets off, cue her with the word, 'Off' then mark the behaviour with 'Yes' and throw another treat to her. (Remember, 'Yes' should always be followed with a food reward).

Step 4. Encourage her to come back to the box and repeat steps 1 and 2, until she is stepping on and off the box with no effort. The cue word can be anything you like, but I use 'Step or Step Up' as my cue.

Make sure you mark the behaviour with 'Yes' and go wild with excitement, when she steps up on to the box with her front paws.

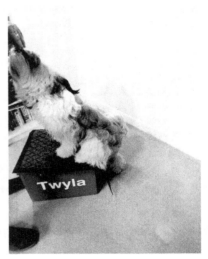

Hide Your Eyes

Cue Word - 'Hide' or 'Hide your Eyes'

This has to be one of the cutest tricks with the biggest aww factor. This takes trust and confidence for your dog, as she has to hide her eyes, which means losing eye contact with you for a few seconds, it may not seem a lot to you, but to your dog, it may be enormous. Many people teach this exercise with the dog putting their paws up on their arm, but I prefer to teach this on an independent object.

We are going to teach it on the box or you can teach it on a chair if you prefer. Personally, I feel it is a much slicker and more professional finish if the dog does it away from you.

Step 1. Your dog needs to have mastered 'Paws Up' in a sit, before attempting this exercise. If you haven't already completed this, go back to teaching this exercise, before continuing.

Step 2. You will need to work very close to your dog, to teach this. Kneel down at the side of the box, with a treat in each hand.

Step 3. Have your dog put her two paws up on the box.

Step 4. Show your dog one of the treats in your hand on the top of the box, while she is concentrating on it, bring your other hand with a treat, behind the box and up between her front paws, if she hasn't spotted it, make a noise to get her attention. It is very important that you bring your hand right through her legs to begin with or she will take her paw of the box to reach the treat. We want to be encouraging her to keep her paws on the box while she feeds.

The aim of the exercise is to have your dog put her muzzle between her paws which will block her vision. The cue is **Hide** or **Hide your Eyes**.

Step 5. Take a lot of time and patience to teach this. Do not rush it. If you try to run before you can walk with this, you will put your dog off and she will lose confidence and trust in you.

Step 6. As your dog gets comfortable placing her muzzle between her paws, gradually decrease how far through her legs you put your hand. This will encourage her to put her head further through which will take her eyes out of sight.

Don't forget to mark the behaviour with a 'Yes' and reward well.

Step 7. Gradually withhold the treat for a few seconds before marking the behaviour with 'Yes' and rewarding. We are aiming to get her to hold the position while she waits for the 'Yes' marker.

Step 8. You now want to hold back on putting your hand between her paws or under her chest, simply point towards the area, from the side of the box and give her the cue 'Hide your eyes'. If she doesn't do it, help her and try again.

Step 9. It is really important that you keep everything positive. Don't get frustrated if she is reluctant, just keep putting your hand through her legs until she is comfortable. The more patient and repetitive you are in helping her she will get it in no time.

Step 10. The final step is to be able to stand back and ask her to 'Hide your Eyes', and keep them hid until you say 'Yes'.

Get On

Cue Word – Get On

The aim of the exercise is for your dog to get on the box and sit down.

A little word about this exercise, once they have learnt this, they tend to choose to do this every time. You need to be sure that you keep control over this, making sure she only gets on it when you tell her to.

Your dog may have no problem with this and do it naturally, other dogs will be very cautious, worried that the box might fall etc. It is very important that you know the box you are using will support your dog's weight and not slide or topple when she gets on it.

Step 1. Hold the treat above the box and encourage your dog with happy tones to get on it. If your dog isn't interested in following the food, take it closer to her and reward for tiny bits of interest, gradually increasing the distance, until she works to get it.

Step 2. Your dog should have already learnt to put her front paws on the box, so she will probably do this bit really quickly, once her two front paws are on it, keep hold of the treat and slowly increase the distance she has to stretch to get it.

Step 3. You will suddenly notice her lift a rear leg towards getting on the box, say 'Yes' to mark the behaviour and reward her. This will confirm for her that, that is what you want.

Step 4. You are nearly there to completing box work, once she gets on the box fully, make a huge fuss with your 'Yes' marker and reward well.

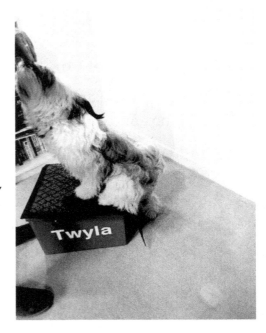

Mr Tibs — Training Tip

Remember your 'Off' cue is crucial to having your dog flow from one exercise to the next, so make sure you reward your Off, or they won't want to do it.

In this Chapter

o Sit High

o Stand High

o Peddling the ball with front feet

Sit High

Cue Word – Sit High

Often referred to as beg, not a term I
particularly like. As a rule, I prefer to call
exercises what they are, say what you
see, Sit High. Some dogs will find this
easier than others, although some of the
dogs I thought would struggle mastered it
easily. One of my biggest surprises was
long backed dogs. I had a Bassett Hound
in one of my classes who was amazing at
this and learnt it in super quick time. It
looked like it was the most natural
position for her to sit in. Some small dogs
usually learn it very quickly, however not
all, some dogs just struggle to get their
balance.

Step 1. With your dog in front of you,
take a treat to her mouth and slowly raise
the treat encouraging your dog to reach
for it, at some point when she is
struggling to reach it, she will lift a paw
from the floor to give her more height,
mark the effort with 'Yes' and reward
her.

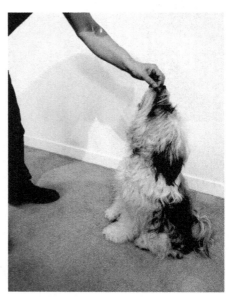

Step 2. Repeat Step 1, as often as you can, Sit High takes a lot of
repetition and a lot of effort for your dog to gain her balance. I always
begin by allowing my dog to balance with her paw around my arm, or

a paw in my hand. This allows her to strengthen her muscles and develop balance from her central core.

You cannot rush this, it has to happen in the dog's time, when she is ready and feels able to do it. It is a great exercise for strengthening their back muscles.

Sensitivity and respect are essential when teaching balancing exercises. Know your dog's capabilities. I had a German Shepherd + Inuit called Ace who took a year to do this on his own. He could sit high really well with my support and I genuinely thought he would never be able to do it unaided and I had accepted that this just wasn't for him. Until one day as I went to help

him and gave the cue 'Sit High', he just did it. I was so excited, I don't think anyone in my class at the time, could understand why I was so excited, given that I was the dog trainer!

It was an enormous achievement for him and to me that he achieved it. He weighed 45kg and I genuinely thought it would never happen. Patience is key.

I find once your dog understands what you want, they try really hard to get it. They will lift their front paws faster and more confidently each time. Initially as you can see from the photos of Rayna as she's learning it, some dogs will bring their paws up really high to gain their balance from you, but the more comfortable and safe your dog feels, they will start to relax their paws, and not lift them so high.

Step 3. Once your dog is sitting high without needing your support, take 1 step back and see if you can get them to do it on cue without any help, again increase your distance slowly, ensuring your dog really gets it and is 100% confident in herself that she can do what you are asking.

Mr Tibs—Training Tip

- The slower you take this exercise, the faster you'll get there.
- Do not try to rush things, your dog must only be asked to do what she is physically capable of doing.

Stand High

This exercise is definitely one that needs careful consideration for each dog. If you have a large heavy dog, it is not wise to be teaching this, as your dog will be taking all their weight on their hind legs and you could cause problems for your dog.

This is a popular exercise/trick that you see used in the canine Heelwork to Music. In my opinion I think it is over used, by over used I mean some dogs spends too long periods of time on their hind legs during one performance. It is not a natural position for a dog to walk like this, so using it in moderation is always advisable.

As a rule, I never teach Stand High, until the dog has mastered Sit High. Teaching Stand High first can make teaching Sit High much more difficult.

Teaching Stand High

Cue Word - Stand High

Strengthening your dog's back leg muscles is essential in order for them to be able to support their body weight and be able to balance. The walking back exercise will help enormously with rear leg muscle development.

Step 1. Begin by having your dog put her paws up high on something, a gate, a fence etc. just teaching her to stand up and balance to begin with, is very important. This will help to give her confidence and strength on her hind legs.

Step 2. You can also use a treat to lure, to encourage your dog to come up on her hind legs to reach it.

Step 3. Once she comes up to reach the treat, you can let her rest a paw on your hand to help her and give her security.

As with 'Sit High', this is another exercise you cannot rush, there are no cutting corners when teaching this. The dog will take as long as she needs to accomplish it. Be patient and understand that regardless of what you think she should be able to do, she may find it difficult.

Peddling the ball with front feet

Cue word – Peddle

Controlling a ball with their front paws is something most dogs would never do naturally. Your dog will need to be confident and trust you. How you introduce the ball to the dog, is crucial. Not getting a fright is super important for your dog and it all rests on you controlling the movement of the ball.

The size of the ball must be appropriate for the size of your dog. I use a Yoga ball for my Tibetan Terriers, it works really-well, but if you have a Yorkshire Terrier, a normal football will probably be big enough. It is important that your dog can reach the top of the ball with their paws and see over it.

Teaching your dog to Peddle the ball

Step 1. Have the ball in front of you and steady the ball with your feet or your knees.

Step 2. Have your dog go behind the ball as she did in box work.

Step 3. Using a treat, lure your dog to step up, i.e. to put her front paws onto the ball. (It is crucial on this first attempt, that the ball does not move as it could frighten the dog and put her off)

Step 4. Repeat these first 3 steps until your dog is comfortably coming up onto the ball and comfortably balancing there.

Step 5. When your dog seems comfortable allow the ball to wobble a little, just enough that she can feel it moving, reward her instantly if she keeps her paws on the ball. If she falls off it, or jumps off it, use a treat to encourage her back onto it.

Step 6. Spend a bit more time just getting her to settle on it.

Step 7. Try again to move the ball ever so slightly, but this time put the treat in front of your dog's mouth, to keep her focus on that and hopefully distract her from what the ball is doing. If she keeps her paws on the ball, while it rocks, make sure you make a huge fuss of her.

Step 8. Use your feet or legs to control the movement of the ball, so that it moves slowly, giving your dog time to feel what she should do with her feet. If it moves too quickly she will most likely panic and not want to get on it again.

Step 9. Your dog will show you what she is capable of as the ball begins to move, expect only short bursts, at first, of the movement with paws up and increase it slowly.

One of my Tibetans, Mosi, is a very confident girl when it came to using objects/props.

When I first started this exercise with her, she would repeatedly try to get on the ball to sit, thinking it was the same as the box work and fell off it so many times at the beginning.

This did not really matter to her as she just loved trying new things out. It didn't take long for her to realise that, that wasn't what I wanted.

She learnt to move the ball in super quick time and was quite proficient at it, albeit a little manic and if you didn't get out of the way she would run you over. She seemed to find this a lot of fun to do.

NOTES

In this Chapter

o Football using their nose
o Circling a bucket with front feet on it
o Targeting an object with their back feet

These exercises require your dog to resist their natural urges. We are going to teach your dog to:

1. Use their nose on an object rather than their mouths or paws.

2. To walk backwards onto an object rather than forward.

3. To circle an object with their front paws up on it.

Confused? Stick with me, all will be explained, and you will have some super cool tricks going on with your dog.

Dog Trainer's Notes

- If you are a dog trainer, your classes will be most impressed when they can demonstrate these super skills their dogs have learnt to their families. Please have a go at them.

- All these exercises work well in the class situation. Don't be daunted by them and don't worry about having to supply all the props. Most owners will prefer their own to practice with. Encourage them to build up their prop bag. Ball, Mat, Touch stick, Bucket, Box, Dumbbell etc.

- It may seem like a lot to bring, but with a little forward planning you can stagger what they bring each week.

Football - using their nose

I start this exercise with a normal football. This was a great exercise for classes to learn, it is great fun for the Training School Christmas Party to have a push the ball relay race or the most balls in a football net.

Any dog can learn to do this. This is a control exercise and demands a lot from the dog mentally in the early stages. The dog is taught to resist all urges to bite or paw the ball. They can only push the ball with their nose.

There are two ways of teaching this.

1. You can teach it, by using the Target Method as you did with the Target Stick. Exchange the target stick for a sticky post-it note, on your hand and then transfer the post it to the ball.

2. However, I prefer to teach it using the treat method, as I find it quicker. The dog will naturally push the ball out of the way to get to the treat. This way, you are working with her instinct, to follow her nose. I find with the post-it note the dog targets it to touch it, rather than push it and they can become a bit frustrated in the early stages if they don't receive a reward for it. In teaching them to push the ball using my method they learn a distinct difference between 'Touch' and 'Push', it is really useful for the dog to know both words as separate exercises for the future, it makes them far more versatile and causes less confusion.

Teaching Push the Ball

Cue word – Push

Step 1. Ask your dog to Sit and Wait. Place the football on the floor and place behind (nearest to the dog) the football a tasty treat, so that your dog can see it.

Step 2. Repeat Step 1, five times.

Step 3. Place the treat further in towards the ball, so that it's barely visible, cue your dog to get it. If the treat was placed correctly, your dog should have accidentally nudged the ball when she went in for the treat. Repeat this

step 5 times and each time introduce the cue word **Push**.

Step 4. This time, ask your dog to Wait; lift the ball, place the treat on the floor and set the ball on top of it, keep one finger on the ball to stop

it rolling off and revealing the treat. Cue your dog to **Push** and as the dog touches the ball allow it to roll away revealing the treat for your dog to eat. Repeat this step 5 times.

Step 5. If your dog is consistent in doing step 4 accurately it's now time to place the treat in front of the ball. Keep your finger or foot on the ball so that it doesn't roll. Cue your dog to 'Push' and as she pushes she should effectively push the ball over the treat to reveal it. Repeat this step 5 times, if she is consistent it's now time to wean her off the treat having to be on the floor. If, however she is not consistent, spend a bit longer placing the treat in front of the ball, before moving onto the next step.

Step 6. Assuming your dog has mastered Step 5, it is time to wean the need for food on the floor. Ask your dog to Sit and Wait. Place the ball in front of her and touch the floor in front of the ball, as though you have placed food there, but don't put food down. The piece of food needs to be in your hand and ready for rewarding.

Step 7. Cue your dog to push and as she pushes the ball, drop the piece of food in front of her on the floor. This helps communicate to your dog, that the food will still be there and to keep her eye on the floor, not looking up at you. Repeat this Step, 5 times and hopefully your dog will be consistent. How quickly you reward will determine the success of this.

Step 8. You are nearly there, it is now time to ask for more than 1 push before feeding, try for 2 then feed, then 3 and feed. Once she reaches this stage, it's time to create some distance between you, the dog and the ball.

Step 9. Start by asking your dog to Sit and Wait, set the ball about a foot in front of her, you stand a couple of feet the other side of the ball. Now point to the ball and ask her to 'Push', if she pushes the ball towards you, mark the behaviour with 'Yes' and throw those treats straight to the floor in front of her. Well done! You have a controlled footballer in the making.

Step 10. Gradually increase the distance between you and the ball, before asking her to push. You can now also increase how many pushes you ask for, before rewarding. Begin with 2 then 3 etc. as she achieves each goal.

Once your dog is proficient at pushing a normal size ball, you can increase and decrease the size of ball, to make it more challenging. In this photo Mosi is pushing a Yoga ball with her nose.

Circling a Bucket with front feet on it.

Cue Word – Step Up and Step Round

The aim of this exercise it to have your dog step up on to an object and circle round it while keeping their paws on it. This involves a lot of work for your dog to use their backend. This is one of my Mosi's favourite exercises and was a firm favourite when I taught it in my classes.

Step 1. To begin teaching this you need a suitable object. Don't use the box that you use for box work. I find it best to use a round object, I use a bucket upside down or a wastepaper bin, or you could even use a round flowerpot. Whatever you choose it is important that it can take the weight of your dog and is strong enough that it won't collapse or fall over easily, when turned upside down, it needs to be wider at the bottom than it is at the top, to make it harder for it to topple over.

Step 2. Stepping up and stepping down. Exactly as you did for stepping up on the box, hold the treat over the centre of the box and encourage your dog to get it. Cue 'Step Up' when your dog attempts it. This should not be hard to

achieve, if your dog already knows it from box work. Repeat 5 times, if your dog has no problems with this, go on to Step 3. If she is hesitant at all, stick with Steps 1 and 2 for another 5 repetitions. She needs to be completely comfortable with the object before moving on.

When a dog is apprehensive about what she is standing on, she will grip with her nails which is more likely to make the surface wobble or even fall, so take your time until she is steady and comfortable, you can even steady the bucket with your feet, until her confidence is better.

Step 3. With your dog's paws on the bucket stand along-side her and hold a treat out in front of her face, as you step into her almost brushing against her side with your legs. You only need to touch her as much as is necessary to encourage her to move out of your space, preferably without getting down from the bucket. As soon as you feel her move her rear end, mark the behaviour with 'Yes' and reward her.

This is another exercise that can take a while to teach, it is a challenge for some dogs and the owner, but it is a great exercise for helping to build your dog's confidence and trust. It is well worth the effort and the pleasure it seems to bring each dog, who masters it.

Step 4. The aim is to get your dog to move all the way round the bucket, while keeping her front paws on it and rear paws on the floor. It is important in

these early stages that your dog keeps her focus straight ahead of her, use the treat to encourage this. If she doesn't reach for the treat her instinct will say to get down off the bucket to go round it.

Step 5. Using your body alongside your dog will encourage her to move round, initially she will be moving to give you space as you move 'into her', but once she has worked out that's what you want her to do, you will no longer need to move with her.

Step 6. It is important to feed her for every step she takes. Give the cue, 'Step Round', repeatedly as you move round together. Repeat these steps as many times as is necessary until your dog is moving round comfortably and effortlessly, with you beside her before trying to get her to move on her own.

Step 7. Using the food still as a lure, hold the food so that your dog turns her head slightly to look at it and ask your dog to Step Round, if she makes one step with her back feet, reward instantly and make a huge fuss. Repeat and repeat until she is doing a full circle of the bucket.

Step 8. Work at building on this slowly, the more confident your dog, the more game she will be to attempt this and the faster she will go.

Two of my dogs, Mosi the Tibetan Terrier and Beanie, the sheep dog, both had no fear of the bucket falling over, both dogs were a little over exuberant doing paw exercises because they had done so many of them, calming them down to go slowly was the hardest bit, so that they didn't knock the bucket down, this was a real challenge for me. Thankfully they knew the word Steady because they are both very fast at everything they do and are very eager to show me they can do it, even when they haven't got a clue. It is a great attitude to work with but one that can cause an accident quickly, if you don't keep it under control.

Targeting with Back Feet

This is a rarely taught exercise in training schools, one that I had great fun teaching in my classes and had great success with it. It is a fantastic exercise for making the dog backend aware, helping them to understand what it is to use their back feet and how to work them when you ask them to. Teaching the Walk Back is a huge start, but it still doesn't teach the dog about targeting just their feet individually. It is quite simple to teach.

All you need is a magazine to begin with.

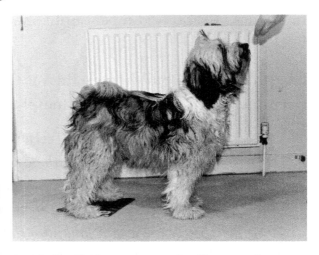

Step 1. Place the magazine on the floor behind your dog and if you have already taught the walk back exercise, ask your dog to walk backwards. If she walks back and touches the magazine even with one foot, mark her success with 'Yes' and reward. Repeat this step and move the goal post 'gradually', until she only gets rewards when both back feet are on it. Remember to add the cue word 'Feet', every time, her feet connect with the target.

There is every possibility that your dog will side-step the dangerous item that is behind her as she will most likely know there is something there that she might crash into and if she wasn't aware of it in the beginning, she will know she has touched it and some dogs will avoid it at all cost next time.

If you have a sensitive dog that is concerned about what is behind her, teach her to walk forward over

the item first. Once she realises she is not going to fall through it or it isn't going to hurt her, she will stop worrying about it. Patience and lots of reward for any connection with it, is usually enough to do the trick.

Step 2. Once your dog is comfortable walking backwards onto the target, you are going to add another magazine or change the object to a thicker book, something like a telephone directory or a catalogue will be ideal. Repeat Step

1 with the new object until she is comfortable with it. Every time she steps onto it, say 'Feet', 'Yes' and reward.

With this thicker book, you will know when she has discovered how to use her back feet, as you send her backwards and say 'Feet', you will see her begin to lift her foot feeling for the book she is stepping onto.

How far you take this exercise is up to you. With Mosi and Beanie they both learnt to back up onto their box, Beanie will attempt to back up onto a wall or anything that is behind her, but Mosi prefers a stand-alone, object like the box.

When I taught this in a class there was one little dog who became a complete star at this exercise, Freddie was so accomplished at using his back feet that he would walk backwards with one foot right up in the air reaching for whatever was behind him, before he even got there. He was extremely skilled at placing his little feet as high up a wall as his little legs would go.

Step 3. To take this to the next level. Simply increase the height of the object you want them to put their feet on. Stairs are a good option for this or a step. Make sure whatever you are asking them to back up onto as it gets higher, is solid and they can't knock it over or it will make them wary of it, as they won't feel they are in control of their safety, particularly as they can't see it.

Thank you!

The purpose of writing this book was not simply because I wanted to produce another book, but because of the memories and joys I have experienced not only from working with my dogs, but from working with other people and their dogs. It is written from my perspective and it is my hope that it will contribute something to the already extensive subject we know as Dog Training.

Being creative, keeping things exciting and encouraging even the most difficult dog to want to work with me and their owners has been what my journey with dogs has been about from the beginning. My hope is by now, you have experienced the thrill of teaching your dog something new or finding new and fun ways to solve whatever frustrating behaviour your dog is presenting you with.

When the weather is against you and your dog is driving you mad because she's bored, please pick up this book and give her something to focus on and make sure she is never short of things to keep her mentally and physically contented.

If you are a trainer, I hope that you have embraced this book in the way in which it is intended. As a supplement to the already wonderful work you are doing, and perhaps it has given you a new twist on some of the exercises you already teach.

Finally, thank you for purchasing this book, I hope it brings you and your dog(s) many hours of fun on your journey together to becoming the perfect companion for each other and the perfect **Clever Canine** team. Happy Training!

Dedication

This book is dedicated to all the dogs that I have had the privilege to know, and to their owners who took the time to understand them to get them help.

For further Dog Training information, you can find me on:

Facebook

- Julie Hindle
- Ace Canine
- Tibetan Terrier Training and Behaviour Workshop
- Tibetan Terrier Grooming and Health Workshop
- Abelenus Tibetan Terriers

Other Dog Training and Behaviour books I have written:

Amazon

Pre-Vaccination Puppy Training
A sure-start guide for you and your puppy

It's Okay to be Alone
A hands-on guide to coping with separation anxiety

Made in United States
North Haven, CT
15 November 2022

26763484R00124